THE LIVING, THE DYING AND THE DEAD

GW00361198

Other books by this author available from New English Library:

THE LIVING, THE DYING AND THE DEAD

George G. Gilman

NEW ENGLISH LIBRARY/TIMES MIRROR

for R. W.
An outsider who nonetheless gets first look

A New English Library Original Paperback, 1978
© by George G. Gilman, 1978

FIRST NEL PAPERBACK EDITION DECEMBER 1978

Conditions of sale: This book is sold subject to the condition that it shall not, by way of trade or otherwise, be lent, re-sold, hired out, or otherwise circulated without the publisher's prior consent in any form of binding or cover other than that in which it is published and without a similar condition including this condition being imposed on the subsequent purchaser.

NEL Books are published by
New English Library Limited from Barnard's Inn,
Holborn, London EC1N 2JR
Made and printed in Great Britain by C. Nicholls & Company Ltd.
Manchester

45003715 0

CHAPTER ONE

THE SKY above Denver had been clear for three weeks but the city and surrounding country still showed evidence of the blizzard which had swept down the Rockies from Montana in the north to the Colorado border with New Mexico Territory in the south. A partial thaw had melted most of the snow where it had simply settled and lain dormant in sheltered areas. But where the wind had swirled and drifted the flakes it was still piled high and was crusted by the frost which ended the thaw – seemed set to maintain its grip on the eastern slopes of the Continental Divide until spring came.

One part of the city completely free from snow, although overlaid like everywhere else by a sun-sparkling carpet of frost crystals, was the Union Pacific railroad depot. But only one train had moved out and none had rolled into the depot since the blizzard hit central Colorado. And although it was close to noon there was very little activity around the lines of stalled cars, the locomotives with cold fireboxes and the buildings which flanked the rails.

A brakeman was checking the couplings on a line of freight cars loaded with iron girders. An engineer was polishing the brass levers in the cabin of his locomotive. A group of heavily coated men stamped their feet and blew into their cupped hands as they peered out along the twin tracks that stretched eastwards from the depot. Three colourfully dressed Orientals emerged from the despatcher's office and moved along a line of boxcars. The man called Edge dropped a half-smoked cigarette and heeled it to shreds into the frosty ground. An old man spat his disgust at this waste of good tobacco.

'Hey, mister! You told me I could have all the butts you were through with!' The old timer's frown cut deeper lines into his face and his voice was high with whining disappointment.

The much taller and younger Edge glanced at his complaining companion and nodded absently. Then, as he returned his attention to the Orientals he unfastened the top two buttons of his black leather coat and reached inside. He drew the makings from his shirt pocket and handed them to the abruptly surprised older man.

'Here.'

'What?'

'Roll yourself a smoke, feller.'

'Gee, thanks.'

'Just the one. Never break my word. Might consider another man's arm if he stole from me.'

The dirty, unshaven and rancid smelling oldster looked briefly up at the profile of his benefactor and realised that what he had just heard was no idle threat. He thought momentarily of giving back the tobacco and papers. But he needed a cigarette more than ever now.

'I'll be inside, mister. Too damn cold out here.'

'I won't miss you until I need another smoke, feller.'

They were standing in front of the open doorway of a small shack on the south side of the depot. It was warm inside, the heat generated by a small stove in a corner. A long table ran down the centre of the shack, flanked by eighteen chairs. Edge, who continued to watch the Orientals moving along the train of boxcars, and the old man who sat down on the chair nearest the stove were all that was left of the eighteen-man snow clearance crew which had been hired by the day to help the regular depot employees. They had been laid off a week ago and were at the depot today because the word was that it was hoped to clear the eastbound track: and both intended to leave Denver on the first available train. They had chosen to wait in the familiar surroundings of the shed rather than the main depot building because a great many other people were anxious to leave the city and neither man liked crowds.

'Here you are, mister. Thanks.'

The tobacco poke was thrust into Edge's unexpectant right hand.

'Obliged,' he said, replacing it in his shirt pocket and re-buttoning his coat without shifting his gaze from the trio of Japanese as they halted beside a car about midway between the locomotive and caboose.

'You know them guys?'

'Seen them a couple of times.'

'Fancy dressers, ain't they?'

With a cigarette to smoke the old man was content again to stand outside in the bright, cold sunlight beside the pre-occupied Edge.

He was right. The three men who slid open the big side door of the boxcar were garbed almost entirely in clothing which emphasised their nationality. They wore long, brightly coloured silken robes and wide brimmed, shallow crowned conical hats. The robes were belted at the waist and each man carried a sword in a curved scabbard hung at his left hip. On the right hip each man wore a Western holster with a Colt revolver nestled inside.

On the two previous occasions Edge had seen the men they had been astride powerful stallions, saddled Western style.

'Friends of yours, mister?'

'Helped me out of a tight spot once.'

There had been nothing furtive about the way the men approached the train and located a particular boxcar. But in cracking open the door and climbing aboard they were cautiously watchful: confident of their right to be where they were but prepared to deal with objectors. Only Edge and the old timer were in a position to see what they were doing and for stretched seconds Oriental and Occidental eyes locked. Three pairs of almond shaped eyes set in the yellow tinged skin of faces which had been weathered by some fifty years of living: faces decorated with thin, drooping, waxed moustaches. One pair of grey, squinting eyes that had seen more than seventy years of life. Looking out of a pale, loose-skinned face, grimed

7

by many days of dirt and stubbled with a week's bristles. And one pair of the lightest blue, slitted narrower than those of the Japanese.

These were the eyes of Edge, their coloration inherited from his Scandinavian mother. At odds with most other features of his face which were drawn from the bloodline of his Mexican father. It was a leanly sculptured face, basically handsome but with an indefinable set – no matter what expression the man wore – which caused many who looked at him to regard it as ugly. The skin, drawn taut between high cheekbones and firm, slightly thrusting jaw, was stained dark by heritage and exposure to the elements. And was scored by more and deeper lines than were merited by the mere passing of close to forty years. The nose was hawklike and the mouth was comprised of wide, thin lips traced along the top and down at each side by a moustache that emphasised the halfbreed's Mexican origins. Also very Mexican was the jet blackness of his thick-growing hair, which he wore long enough to brush his shoulders.

It was a face in which many of the lines cutting away from the eyes and mouth told of past suffering. While the cold glint in the hooded eyes and the set of the mouth warned of the cruel streak which the man had developed as a result of his experiences. A face which seldom smiled, unless with bitter humour: and which could strike icy fear into the heart of anyone who had offended the man called Edge.

His frame was built on the same lean lines as his face for although he weighed in the region of two hundred pounds, the dark toned flesh was firmly moulded to the bones.

He was clothed in a low crowned grey Stetson, a black leather jacket over a grey shirt, black pants and black, spurless riding boots. Around his waist was a worse-for-wear gunbelt with a tied down holster on the right. His jacket was rucked up on that side, to allow him access to the Remington revolver which jutted from the holster. A straight razor, which was as deadly a weapon as the gun, was concealed in a leather pouch which hung down under his shirt from the nape of his neck: held in place by a beaded leather thong worn beneath his grey kerchief.

He inclined his head slightly and briefly, as a sign of recognition rather than friendliness, when one of the Japanese did a double take toward him and gestured for the other two to do the same. This was the only clue that the recognition was mutual before the door of the boxcar was slid almost closed.

'Hey, them guys don't look like they need to ride freight trains,' the old timer growled.

'You work for the railroad anymore, feller?'

'You know I don't.'

'So it's none of your business.'

The filthy, unshaven face showed a pained expression. 'Just makin' talk is all, mister. Anyways, you been eye ballin' them as much as I have.'

'That's none of your business either.'

'Pardon me for friggin' livin'!' the old man snarled, and drew a final iota of satisfaction from the last shreds of tobacco before he abandoned the tiny butt to the frosty ground.

'Granted,' Edge answered, his cold blue eyes shifting in their slitted lids to locate a wagon as it rolled into the depot between a pair of gates.

'You ain't the easiest guy in the world to get along with, are you?'

The half-breed pursed his lips and sighed softly. 'We shovelled some snow together, feller. That doesn't have to make us bosom buddies, does it?'

'You don't want me around, is that it?'

'You any use to me?'

The old man expressed injured pride, then scorn and, finally, pity. Edge saw none of these facial changes for he continued to watch the slow moving wagon as it was steered over a series of timber track crossings and then along the side of the line of boxcars. It was an enclosed market wagon pulled by two black horses and driven by a hard-eyed young man in his early twenties. There was tension in the way he sat the wagon seat and suspicion in the way he tried to keep watch on every part of the depot at once.

'If you live to be as old as me, maybe you'll learn it don't do a guy no harm to have friends, mister!'

The pity was gone by the time Edge glanced again at the old timer: to be replaced by disappointment.

'You seemed like a right guy to me. My mistake.'

'Yeah, feller,' the half-breed said to the stoop-shouldered back of the old man as he started away from the shack toward the group of railroad men waiting at the start of the eastbound track. 'You're right. I'm wrong.'

Then Edge moved away from the doorway and began to step over rails and ties, on a catty-cornered course toward the boxcar in which the Japanese were concealed. He knew, without being able to see them, that the Orientals were watching his advance. Perhaps as intently as the hard-eyed young man driving the enclosed wagon. The half-breed halted, one track away from the almost closed door of the boxcar, and waited for the wagon to roll past him and come to a stop: its rear level with one side of the door.

'We don't need no help,' the driver growled, remaining in his seat as he leaned to the side and looked back. 'And all the paperwork's been done if that's what bothers you.'

'Who's we, feller?' Edge asked evenly.

The wagon had a tailgate with double doors above. The latch was raised from the inside and the doors folded open gently, pushed by the hands of a man slightly older than the driver. He was dressed in the same city style as the man up front – grey derby, dark blue suit and white shirt with a black bow tie at the collar. In one of his hands he held a double barrelled shotgun. The sound of the driver climbing down off the wagon caught Edge's attention and he saw that the younger man was now carrying a similar gun. When the half-breed shifted his eyes back to the man in the rear of the vehicle, he saw that this one now held his gun in both hands. Neither weapon was aimed at Edge. But two pairs of dark eyes in pale faces warned that the situation could quickly alter.

'Him and me,' the man in the rear answered.

Edge nodded stoically. 'The fellers in the boxcar out-number you, but I figure those shotguns even the odds.'

The driver had reached the back of the wagon. So that both were in a position to snap their heads around and swing their guns: to aim at the door of the boxcar as it was rolled open.

'We wish not to kill nor to die.'

'Just to have back what is ours.'

'You are innocents who have been duped.'

The trio of Japanese stood in a line in the open doorway of the car. Their round, sallow complexioned faces were expressionless and their arms were akimbo: hands far away from the hilts of the swords and butts of the Colts.

'Hold it, Luke!' the man in the rear of the wagon snapped.

'I am, Brad. But damnit, I almost let them have both barrels.'

The centrally placed Japanese in the line shifted his attention to Edge who continued to stand with surface casualness on the far side of the sun-glinting rails. 'Unless you have hidden motive, we are all indebted to you, sir. We did not think the casket would be so heavily guarded. Your warning has saved lives.'

'It's a trick!' Luke snarled. 'Cover the tall guy, Brad!'

Edge drew the Remington in a shockingly fast series of movements: all of them linked smoothly together. His right hand reached for the butt and slid the gun from the holster. The hammer was cocked before the barrel was clear of the leather. And the muzzle was trained on Brad's narrow back before the young man had swung his head.

There was still a veneer of the casual about the half-breed's stance. But his gaze was as rock steady and as threatening as the revolver in his brown skinned fist. The blue slivers of his slitted eyes seemed impossibly cold, perhaps inhuman. And the total lack of emotion in them acted to freeze Brad where he stood, with just his head turned to look back over his left shoulder. The man opened his mouth to speak, but Edge's voice sounded first.

'I'm not in the business of saving lives,' he said evenly, and saw Luke chance a fast, anxious glance at him before returning his attention to the unmoving, implacable Japanese. 'But words cost me nothing. Anyone points a gun at me better squeeze the trigger right off. Or I'll kill him, sooner or later.'

The warning given, he pushed the Remington back into the holster. As smoothly as he had drawn it, but much more slowly.

Brad kept his mouth open for long enough to draw in a deep breath. The fresh, bitingly cold air in his lungs did little to dispel the fear which had gripped him when he found his eyes locked with those of Edge.

'Just what is your business here?' Luke asked tensely, guessing from the sounds behind him and Brad's reactions that the revolver was back in the holster.

'It's finished now,' the half-breed answered. 'A favour's been returned. Never like to feel beholden to people.'

Two of the Japanese were as puzzled as Luke and Brad. But the one in the centre, who had the scar tissue of an old knife wound along his right jaw line gave a curt nod of understanding.

'We saved your life far to the north of here. You consider you have saved ours, sir.'

'Three for one, feller. But let's not get into counting heads.'

'If we did, there were many more than one aboard the boat, sir,' the scarred Japanese countered.

'Only one that mattered,' Edge responded as he turned away from the boxcar and wagon. 'To me.'

He retraced his footsteps back across the rails and ties toward the shack and sensed three pairs of eyes watching him from behind.

'Okay, get down out of that car!' Luke demanded. 'And beat it!'

'Can we not come to some arrangement, sir? We are prepared to pay a reasonable price to have returned to us that which is ours.'

'You don't get outta here damn fast, we'll blast you!' Brad

warned, his anger powered by remembered fear. 'And the law'll be on our side.'

The brakeman had completed his chore of checking couplings on the far side of the depot. The engineer had run out of brass to polish. And, like the old timer, they had gone to join the group of trainmen watching for the return of the locomotive and four cars despatched earlier to check if the eastbound track was open. If anyone but Edge was aware of the levelled shotguns at the boxcar, they were watching from cover.

By the time the half-breed got back to his vantage point at the doorway of the shack, the Orientals had submitted to the threat of the guns. They were down off the train and moving away from the rear of the wagon. They did not look back or at Edge. Instead, straight ahead. At the end of the train they altered course and went toward the main depot building. But they did not enter it — went from sight around one side of it. Both Luke and Brad watched them all the way, crouching down on their haunches so that they could see the lower halves of the Orientals' robes under the stalled cars of the trains. Only when they were certain the trio had left the depot did they spare a hostile glance for Edge: and spotted him in process of lighting a freshly rolled cigarette as he leaned against the doorframe of the shack.

Brad said something which drew a shrug from Luke. Then they got to work, still carrying the shotguns as they tugged at harness and cursed at the horses – manoeuvring the wagon so that its open rear was hard against the doorway of the boxcar. There was a gap at the side and they climbed up through it. The tailgate banged against the floor of the car and after this whatever sounds the two men made were not loud enough to carry to Edge. But he did see the wagon rise on its springs as something heavy was dragged into the car.

A clock across the street from the main depot building began to strike the midday hour. The two men jumped down from the car before the final chime sounded. While Brad climbed up on the seat and eased the wagon forward a few yards, Luke

13

raked his eyes around the depot, going down on his haunches again to peer beneath the cars. Then, satisfied that Edge was the only man watching him, he slid the boxcar door closed and shuttered the rear of the wagon.

He thudded the stock of his shotgun on a side panel and Brad started the horses forward. The wagon had to be driven a hundred yards out ahead of the locomotive coupled to the line of boxcars before Brad found a crossing where he could get over the many sidetracks. Luke watched his partner for a few moments, then used the iron rung ladder at the rear of the boxcar to climb up on the roof. Bright sunlight, still not warm enough to melt the frost, glinted on the oiled barrels of the shotgun as he swung this way and that, maintaining a hard eyed vigil over the white layered depot.

The wagon's route to the gateway took it immediately across the front of the shack where Edge stood, his thumbs hooked over the buckle of his gunbelt now that the cigarette was finished. He watched the approaching wagon with complete indifference. But the city-suited young man on the seat did not trust this attitude and drove with one hand on the reins and the other fisted around the frame of the cocked shotgun. There was a slight sheen of nervous sweat on his cheeks and hat-shaded forehead. His eyes were constantly shifting, moving to the full extent of their sockets as he divided his fearful attention between the relaxed half-breed and the tense figure of Luke atop the boxcar.

Until the beat of galloping hooves filled the crisp, midday air: abruptly masking the creak and clop of the wagon and team's progress.

Brad, Luke and Edge all swung their heads toward the source of the new sound. In time to see the riders wheel their mounts in through the gateway at the western end of the depot. The three Japanese, as perfectly aligned astride their horses as they had been standing in the boxcar. Each controlling his animal with reins held in one hand while the other was fastened around the frame of a repeater rifle.

Puffs of white smoke spurted from the muzzles.

14

Brad yelled: 'You sneaky bastard!'

Luke squeezed both barrels of his shotgun.

The roar of both barrels exploding their loads masked the sharper cracks of the rifles.

Bystanders shouted their shock at the abrupt outbreak of unexpected violence. Some in the group at the start of the eastbound track hurled themselves to the ground. Doors of many buildings were flung open. Faces appeared at several windows.

Luke did not see the scattering shot from his twin barrelled gun fall far short of the moving targets. For two rifle bullets had hit him. One in the stomach, the other in the centre of his forehead. Blood soaked his suit jacket from the lower wound: gushed out to drench his eyes with liquid crimson from the upper one. He staggered backward for several drunken paces, dropping the empty gun. Then became limp in death and fell hard between two boxcars, his corpse folding over the coupling.

Brad was dead before his partner's body came to rest.

His accusation had been hurled at Edge as the half-breed had drawn the Remington – the move an instinctive one to the sound of gunfire. Brad dropped the reins as he shouted, and got two hands on the shotgun. Edge was in a gunfighter's crouch, sideways on to the galloping Japanese and in the process of aiming from the hip. The two horse team continued to maintain the easy pace. The rifle bullet intended for Brad missed his head by less than an inch as he leaned to the side to draw a bead on Edge.

The half-breed turned his head at the sound of Brad's voice. Just as the front of the wagon came level with him. The twin muzzles of the shotgun were made to appear enormous by the fear which gripped Edge. A very real fear of being ripped apart by a double load of shot. But a cold, controlled fear. Far removed from terror. A fear that acted to hone his mental and physical reflexes. Speeded them to assure that he would be the winner in this latest kill or be killed contest.

The swing of his gun hand was almost as fast as the rake

of his eyes. And skill took up where reflex ended. He knew precisely at which point in the arc to halt his hand. Then his index finger squeezed the trigger. He made just the right allowances for the recoil of the Remington. Then hurled himself to the ground to the side.

He did not see the gory hole appear where Brad's right eye had been. Nor the blast of acrid smoke from the twin muzzles of the shotgun as a dying nerve caused the man's finger to pull against the triggers. Merely heard the explosion and the impact of the shot against the front of the timber shack.

The two horses in the traces continued on their way, apparently impervious to the blast.

Edge had hit the frost layered ground on his belly. He rolled on to his back and sat up. He saw Brad had dropped the shotgun off the wagon and that the man's arms, head and shoulders were hanging over the side. Droplets of blood splashed down to mark a parellel course with the tracks of the wheels.

Peering beneath the wagon and then around it as it ceased to be an obstacle, he saw that the three Japanese were still racing their mounts across the treacherous rails and ties. Heading for the boxcar where Luke had died.

Men were shouting and women were screaming. The group which had been watching for the return of the first train out had scattered in frantic search of cover.

The scar-faced Oriental looked briefly toward Edge and nodded curtly: much as the half-breed had done earlier as a sign of recognition.

The wagon bounced over a hump in the ground and the corpse of Brad was shaken loose. The man's arms remained above his head and the rear wheels of the vehicle bounced again: accompanied by a double crack as both wrists were crushed between iron rims and frozen soil.

Edge showed a fleeting scowl. Then was impassive as he powered to his feet. The three Japanese were almost at the boxcar, reining their horses to a halt. They were beyond effective revolver range, but the half-breed squeezed off three shots. Two of the bullets ricocheted off rails and the third imbedded itself in a tie. The gunfire and its following sounds were enough to freeze the Japanese as they prepared to dismount. Shock at the apparent turnabout in Edge's loyalty caused them to hesitate. Gave the half-breed time to achieve the cover of the inside of the shack.

Then the scar-faced man shouted an order in his native language. And the other two exploded rifle fire at the shack: still in their saddles as the man who had given the command leapt to the ground and lunged toward the boxcar door.

Edge's bedroll and saddle, with a Winchester rifle in the boot, was leaning against the wall just inside the doorway of the shack. He pulled the rifle clear and stayed flat on the floor until the fusillade of shots ended. Then rose behind the window.

His face had been impassive when he killed Brad — a true facial image of his feelings. For the shot he fired then had been an act of self-defence. This was different. He had returned a favour and his intentions had been misconstrued. As a result of which he had been required to gun down a man who meant nothing to him: in front of countless witnesses. So now he had to even the score. The code by which he lived demanded it.

There was unmistakable ugliness in his face now, as he thrust forward the Winchester to smash the window at the same instant as he squeezed the trigger. The ugliness of brutal cruelty in the way his lips curled back from his teeth, the skin stretched drum taut across his bone structure and his eyes narrowed to threads of glinting blueness beneath the hooded lids. Evil emanated from every pore and line in his face.

And a Japanese died. One of those who were mounted. He was hit in the throat, by a bullet which had enough velocity to penetrate tissue and bone: emerging at the back in a ghastly spray of blood and gristle chips.

The dead man was flung off his saddle, crashed against the side of the boxcar and slammed to the ground. His horse reared in response and the animal's flailing forehooves struck the mount of the other man who had remained in the saddle.

17

The horse snorted and bolted. The man released his rifle in his anxiety to grasp the reins and stay astride the animal.

The scar-faced Japanese had slid the door of the boxcar half open when the killing shot was fired. He saw its effect and wasted what could have been a fatal stretched second in staring at the man standing behind the shattered window. If he expected to die, his expression showed no fear of it. Then there was only bemusement on his face as he saw Edge make a sideways gesture with the rifle. It was intended, and taken, as a sign of dismissal. His own horse had remained calm: and responded in a well schooled manner when the man swung smoothly up into the saddle and demanded an immediate gallop.

The bolting horse had carried its rider to the start of the eastbound track before the man regained control. This was the direction the second surviving Oriental took, Winchester clear of the boot against the possibility that other men in the depot might not be so accommodating as Edge.

Even after the two riders had gone from sight beyond a thick stand of timber which bordered the eastern side of the Union Pacific depot, nobody stepped out into the open. Until Edge showed himself. Empty handed: the rifle back in the boot and the revolver in its holster.

Then they advanced from their cover. Men mostly, but a few women emerged from the main building. Some shock was expressed, in looks and words; but mostly the crowds which gathered by the boxcar and around the slumped form of Brad were morbidly curious.

Only the rancid smelling old timer ventured to approach Edge. 'Gee, mister,' he croaked. 'Whose side are you on?'

'Mine,' the half-breed answered as some uniformed figures showed at a door in the main depot building – not all of them in Union Pacific livery. In the centre of the group was a red faced man of advanced years who gestured a great deal with his hands as he talked fast to those around him. But nobody seemed to be listening to him.

The group halted briefly at the boxcar with one body at the

18

side of it and another folded over the coupling, then continued across the tracks toward Edge. The old timer backed hurriedly away in the face of advancing officialdom.

Four of the men were Union Pacific employees, expressing anxiety. Three more were attired in the uniforms of the Denver City Police Department. As they came to a halt in front of the shack, the policeman with most braid on his jacket waved the talkative old man into silence. And the two junior men matched the glowering look which he directed at Edge.

'Figure you fellers want to know what happened?' the half-breed asked evenly.

'I know what happened, mister!' the senior man snarled, bending a thumb and stabbing it against his chest. 'Three men just got shot dead. But you can bet your ass I want to know what kinda game you think you're playin'!'

Edge curled back his lips to show a grin that might have been warm if the expression had spread high enough to melt the coldness in his narrowed eyes. 'Guess it's more than my ass that's on the line, chief,' he growled between his clenched teeth. 'On account that this is something bigger than a crap game.'

CHAPTER TWO

EDGE told his story in the stove heated, tobacco smoke smelling office of the despatcher. His audience was comprised of the granite featured Denver police chief, the two young constables, the agitated depot manager and the red faced old man who had been driven into resentful silence with a warning that he would have to stay outside unless he kept quiet. His face — the colour of boiled lobster — was the only one which did not express some degree of hostility as the half-breed folded his long, lean frame into the despatcher's padded chair and waited for the others to settle themselves.

For a reason he could not even guess at, Edge had been allowed to keep the Remington. The two constables either did not know the reason, or mistrusted it: for both draped hands over the butts of their own holstered Colts.

Outside the breath-misted window of the office, the depot was almost deserted again, the groups of curious bystanders having dispersed after the corpses were moved into the temporary mortuary of an unheated locomotive shed.

There was no sign yet of the train which had been sent out to check on snow conditions to the east of the city.

'All right, Mr ...' The chief looked at the depot manager, who had given Edge a job on the snow clearance crew.

'Edge,' the nervous, somewhat effeminite man supplied. 'That's the only name he gave.'

The police chief nodded and returned his attention to Edge. 'Impress me, mister,' he invited sourly.

The old man looked anxious, then seemed for a few moments to be trying to express some tacit message across the small, over-crowded office. But Edge met his eyes only fleetingly and gave no indication that he was drawing any conclusions from the faces pulled at him. And he was not, for he had already had a strong hunch of just where the old man fitted into this situation.

Instead, he devoted his empty eyed attention to the uniformed police chief, who seemed about as easy to impress as he was himself.

'It starts with an unborn baby a lot of people thought was going to be Jesus Christ,' he opened, and succeeded even in jolting the hard faced man out of his cynical composure.

But the police chief recovered fast. He shifted his rump into a more comfortable position on a cluttered side table and growled: 'You figurin' to plead insanity, mister?'

'Guess I did go a little crazy up there,' Edge admitted absently as his mind brought forward recollections of events a few short weeks ago amid the snow covered peaks of Wyoming's Wind River Mountains.

It was there that he had first seen the three strangely dressed Japanese, at a time when he and several other people were affected by a series of happenings that paralleled those of the Nativity. At the dangerous crossing of a swollen river in flood. When those aboard the helpless ferry might well have died had the trio of Orientals not appeared, to throw them a lifeline.

For a while, the whole episode over that Christmas Eve and Christmas Day had profoundly affected the man called Edge: and in retrospect he found it reassuring to consider that he took part in the strange affair of the never-to-be second coming as a result of some inexplicable mental aberration. Reassuring because it was totally alien to his nature to be influenced by the fervour of a bunch of religious fanatics. Alien — and dangerous — for a man like Edge to be affected by any influence outside his own desire for survival. For he was a man destined to exist always on the narrow line between harsh life and violent death.

Perhaps it had always been like that, even as a child. Although there had been nothing unique about his family circumstances. He was the elder of two brothers who lived with

21

their parents on a small farmstead in Iowa. His name then had been Josiah Carl Hedges and he spent his early years under threat of crop failure at best and Plains Indian attack at worst.

He and his brother, Jamie, had survived and after the deaths of their mother and father there had seemed no reason why they should not have continued to make a good living on the Iowa prairie. Even though the younger Hedges boy was crippled as the result of a gunshot accident for which Josiah was responsible.

But war came and it was mutually decided that the able-bodied brother should leave to fight for the Union army against the rebels of the south. He entered the long and bloody War Between the States as little more than a callow youth and was discharged as a man. A man who had learned to hate and to kill — and to kill even if there was no reason to hate.

But, like many others, he rode away from the battlegrounds of the east toward the unscarred fields of the west firmly resolved to forget the past and make a golden future. Until he found the farm a charred ruin and the tortured body of Jamie in the yard.

Impulse — perhaps insanity? — had possessed him then. And he rode away from the farmstead determined to avenge the brutal murder of his brother. Fully aware of the identities of the men for whom he searched. Five of the most vicious troopers who had fought for the Union — who had ridden under his command for most of the war. He found them and, using his war-taught skills, killed them. But in his reckless thirst for revenge he also killed a man who did not, perhaps, deserve to die. And the Kansas authorities issued flyers which stated that former Captain Josiah C. Hedges was wanted for the murder of Elliot Thombs.

Thus had Hedges become Edge, unpunished by the law but made to suffer harshly by a destiny that dictated he must be a drifter, a loner and a loser. Riding the trails of the western states and territories with no other aim than to simply stay alive.

At first he had attempted to beat his fate — to put down roots, form friendships and grasp some of the good things of life. But always such efforts were doomed to failure: inevitably to the brutal accompaniment of violent death and wanton destruction.

It was during that post-war period that he had been made to suffer most. For he had grown to like, and in one case love, some of those who died. And to consider that he had a right to own that which he so fleetingly possessed.

But in the aftermath of the death of his wife — had he been insane to marry Beth? — he came to terms with his destiny. By realising that if he desired nothing or no one, owned nothing and formed no attachment to anyone then he could not be made to endure grief or even a sense of loss.

He had adjusted to the terrors and horrors of war by hardening himself into such an attitude, and it was relatively easy to do so again after the tragic way in which Beth died.

So, although violence continued to dog his back trail or to lay in wait for him, he was almost always on his guard against it: and could deal with it without the need to consider anything except his own survival. Almost always: because even in the time since Beth died he had been tempted on occasions to feel other than the most base of human emotions. Most recently up in the Wind River Range when he had allowed himself to be infected by the mass hysteria — madness? — generated by the birth of a baby.

But even when such a thing happened and the inevitable end resulted, the man called Edge emerged mentally unscathed. Feeling only self-anger that he had allowed himself to become involved emotionally with other people. For to be so enmeshed in the lives of others meant he was not totally devoted to his personal survival. And because of the narrow line he was forced to walk this was dangerous.

Without going into detail about the surrounding events, Edge told the granite featured police chief how the trio of Japanese had maybe saved his life. How they had asked questions about a man named Silas Martin. How he had last seen the three brightly attired men riding south. How he had ridden south, to reach Denver just ahead of the big snow.

When he named Silas Martin he saw that his hunch had been correct. For the old man accompanied a curt nod with a fleeting smile. Then the half-breed told one more truth and embroidered it with lies.

'It seemed to me that those three fellers weren't looking for Martin to ask about his state of health. And when I saw them hide out in the boxcar just before the wagon showed up with freight I figured I might get a job with more prospects than shovelling snow.'

The old man's nod was more emphatic this time. He was almost excited.

'There's not much prospects at the end of a rope, mister,' the police chief growled, and looked as if he wanted to spit in disgust. 'The foreigner you killed was up to no good, that's for sure. But you also knocked off Brad Sinclair. He was with the Denver Security Express Company. Working for Mr Martin here.'

'His mistake, chief,' Edge answered. 'I owed those Orientals for saving my life up in Wyoming. Sinclair and his partner were too nervous and nervous men carrying shotguns are dangerous. So I refereed a truce situation at the boxcar. When the fellers in the fancy clothes came back shooting, Sinclair figured I was with them. It was him or me, with no time for talk.'

There was something else that had a bearing on the killing of Brad Sinclair – the fact that he had aimed a gun at Edge after being told not to. One of the half-breed's few idiosyncrasies, stemming from that terrible day in his youth when he had pointed what he thought was an unloaded Starr rifle at Jamie and crippled his younger brother for the rest of his short life.

Edge did not add this.

'You satisfied, Chief Sorrel?' Silas Martin demanded into the hard, lengthening silence. 'It's like I told you. And like at least twenty other witnesses will tell you. This man drew against the Japanese but had to defend himself against Sinclair.'

Sorrel sighed wearily as he shoved himself off the table and went to clear a patch of mist off the window to peer out across the depot. 'I ain't never satisfied after there's been killin's in my city, mister,' he replied sourly. 'Especially when some fast-gun, trigger-happy stranger is involved. And it's a law-abiding local citizen that's spilled his blood on Denver soil. But I guess I'm gonna have to let this one stay stuck in my craw and go out after them fancy threaded foreigners.'

He turned away from the window to scowl his disgust at Edge, who met the expression with a flat, empty gaze.

'But there's a condition to that, mister. Martin here will leave with his crate just as soon as we get word the line east is open. You got to be aboard the first train out as well.'

'Figured to be, chief,' the half-breed said.

Silas Martin slid off the high stool on which he had been perched. His face was not such a vivid colour now. 'Of course he will, Chief Sorrel. How can he stand guard over my poor wife unless he is with her?'

Edge's usually impassive eyes showed a flicker of surprise. 'Your wife, feller?'

'Didn't you know?' His surprise was more expressive. 'Yes, the crate delivered to the depot by the express company contains a casket in which are the remains of my poor wife.'

'Havin' second thoughts, Edge?' Sorrel asked sardonically as he made for the door and the young constables vied for the privilege of opening it for him. 'Standin' sentry duty over a corpse?'

The half-breed shrugged his broad shoulders as a train whistle screeched to the east of the city. 'No sweat, chief. What's wrong with being a bodyguard?'

CHAPTER THREE

Silas Martin was aged between sixty-five and seventy and carried his years well. He stood little more than five feet three inches tall but made the most of it by keeping his back straight and his head held high. His belly bulged and his face was fleshy but he was not grossly overweight. The grey hair on his head was thin, but the sideburns he wore down to each side of his jaws grew bushy. His eyes under jutting brows were brown with clear surrounds. His nose was too broad and his mouth did not seem wide enough. His looks were pleasantly avuncular.

He was dressed in a mourning suit which had seen better days, the pants shiny on the seat and the jacket frayed at the cuffs. He suffered from a compulsion to talk all the time.

'You're a fast thinking young man, I like that,' he said the moment they were out of the main depot building, their expelled breath forming white vapour in the bitter cold of early afternoon. 'I've been a fast thinker all my life. A man has to keep one step ahead of the opposition. But it's no good doing anything until you've thought about it.'

Edge blew into cupped hands, feeling the cold worse than before after enjoying the warmth of the despatcher's office. The frost-covered depot was no longer deserted and many others who had emerged from the heated buildings were also fighting the chill air — blowing in their hands, stamping their feet and slapping their arms in front of them. But they endured the discomfort gladly, eager to learn as soon as possible about snow conditions east of Denver.

A few people were held inside against their will, as Chief Sorrel and the two constables questioned them: going through the motions of confirming that Edge had shot Brad Sinclair in self-defence. But they were released from their obligations as eye-witnesses in time to hurry outside and watch the return of the train.

It was comprised of a locomotive with a Buckner snow-plough fitted to the front, hauling four boxcars filled with men and equipment, and a caboose. The train reversed into the depot on the main track and was switched to a side line: so it was the brakeman who was the first of the crew to be seen. And his broad grin and the way he held both hands clasped above his head revealed that the line to the east was open.

Passengers cheered and then rounded on harassed Union Pacific officials to fire questions about departure times.

Edge clucked his tongue against the roof of his mouth and started out across the tracks toward the shack to collect his gear. Silas Martin was talking again, as fast as ever, and did not realise the half-breed was moving until he was several feet away. He had to run to catch up with the taller, younger man.

'Hey, you meant what you said about wanting to work for me, didn't you?' he asked, his colour high again from anxiety rather than exertion.

'Sure, feller. I travel light, but not this light.'

'Of course. Your baggage. What about payment? How would five dollar a day suit?'

'I'm going east anyway. Nobody was going to pay me for it until I ran into you.'

'All the way to New York?'

'It's a place I've never been.'

'Then we have a deal?'

The half-breed's voice took on a tone of irritation. 'You want it in writing, feller?'

Martin shook his head. 'No. No, Mr Edge. It's just that I can hardly believe my luck. Meeting up with a man like you.'

'Don't count on it holding.'

Martin's flushed and fleshy face showed anxiety. 'You mean . . . ?'

'Just that. Nobody wins them all.'

Now the old man smiled, showing teeth that were too perfect

27

to be natural. 'You perhaps have good reason to be a pessimist, Edge. But throughout my life I have lost little of consequence.'

'Except a wife?' the half-breed suggested evenly as they stepped across the last pair of rails and closed in on the shack.

Martin ceased to smile but his tone of voice did not indicate depression. 'A fatal disease is not a matter of luck. Simply a process of natural selection.'

There was a great deal of noise throughout the depot: as freight was trundled towards waiting trains, passengers boarded and crewmen worked eagerly to build up heads of steam in their locomotives. So it was not until Edge stepped across the threshold of the shack that the two men inside became aware of him — and he of them. He halted abruptly and Silas Martin collided with him and vented a short cry of alarm.

'Damnit, it's him!' the old man who smelled bad rasped.

'So what?' a much younger man with red hair and a beard muttered.

They had been down on their haunches close to the half-breed's gear. The old man unfurling the bedroll and the younger one delving into a saddlebag.

'What's going on?' Martin demanded, suddenly perturbed.

'Daylight robbery,' Edge answered flatly. And stepped into the shack, back kicking the door closed in Martin's face.

The malodorous old man slammed hard on to his rump in his haste to rise from his haunches. His partner, as ill clothed and bad smelling, had the youthful agility to power smoothly up into an aggressive crouch. His right hand went from sight behind his back, and reappeared fisted around the handle of a slim-bladed knife. He held his well balanced stance for a fraction of a second. Then formed his hirsute face into a snarl and lunged forward.

Edge could have drawn the Remington and blasted a bullet into his attacker. But he did not trust the granite faced Chief Sorrel to accept attempted robbery as mitigation for the result of a gunshot against a knife. So he streaked his own right hand into the hair at the nape of his neck. He also raised his left hand at the same time.

Which disconcerted the man with the knife: who perhaps saw the raised hands as a sign of surrender. Until the half-breed's right hand came down and forward, clutching the open straight razor.

The knife was on target for a vicious underarm stab into Edge's belly. But the man's eyes, puzzled and then angry, were focused on the gleaming blade of the razor.

The half-breed remained with his back to the closed door for a stretched second, his dark skinned face showing nothing of what he felt as the bearded man closed with him. Then he snapped from defence to counter-attack without a sound or look of warning: as composed as a man mildly irritated at the belligerence of a spoiled child. But the punishment he dealt out was harsher.

He swung sideways-on as the point of the knife came within three inches of his exposed stomach. Crouched down to avoid the man's left hand which clutched at his right wrist. And shot forward his own left hand to grasp a great turf of the red beard.

His assailant, who was short but solidly built, vented a roar of rage that became tinged with pain as his facial hair was yanked. He came to a halt and tried to back off, arcing his knife hand away to start a new stabbing movement.

But Edge had no need to change his tactics. His right hand was in position to begin an upward swing, between his own and his attacker's bodies — under his left forearm to sink the blade of the razor deep into the armpit of the other man.

The bearded man grunted as he felt a mild discomfort in the area of the wound. Then screamed, in realisation of what was happening rather than in pain, as the blade was withdrawn for half its length: to be slashed downward from armpit to elbow before it came free of his blood gushing flesh.

The knife slipped from his swinging hand and suddenly he was sent staggering backward, to crash across the long table: driven into helpless retreat by the half-breed's left hand, which released the beard only to claw at the upper face and shove at it. With enough force to slide the wounded man over the table and hard to the floor on the other side.

'It was Clyde's idea, sir!' the evil smelling old man whined. 'Clyde figured you might have some liquor.'

He started out talking to Silas Martin, who was aiming a tiny gun at him through the shattered window of the shack. But finished up directing his fear-filled gaze and quivering words at Edge as the impassive half-breed stepped toward him.

'On your belly, feller,' the tall, lean man said flatly. 'Right arm out to the side.'

The old timer swallowed hard and a tear swelled at the corner of each eye to spill down his cheeks. 'What you gonna do to me?'

'What I told you I would.'

The terrified man was still down on his rump, where he had been held by the threat of Martin's gun.

'Oh, my God, I'm bleedin' to death,' Clyde groaned as he pulled himself up on to a chair and flopped his bloodsoaked arm across the table top. His beard no longer looked so vividly coloured. Beneath the dirt ingrained into his cheeks and foreheard his skin was waxen and white.

'So best you make your peace with Him, feller,' the half-breed growled. 'Right now I've got a bone to pick with your partner.'

The old timer trembled as the razor was lowered toward him. But Edge simply wiped both sides of the crimson dripping blade on the man's coat shoulder before replacing the weapon in the neck pouch. Then the man screamed, and screamed again. First when he was gripped by the coat lapels and dragged up and flung down, his chin crashing against the floorboards of the shack. The second time when Edge broke his right arm — by setting a foot on the elbow and jerking the wrist up. The bone snapped with a sickening crack, creating enough pain to sink the old man into a faint, curtailing his scream.

'Was that necessary?' Silas Martin asked, as a straightforward question with no criticism implied in his expression or tone of voice.

'He got a warning,' Edge replied, as he crouched to refurl his bedroll and fasten the straps on his saddlebags.

'We figured you'd be on your way to the city gaol,' Clyde rasped through teeth clenched against pain.

'Lots of people make mistakes,' the half-breed replied.

The injured man managed to sneer with his mouth and hate with his eyes. 'But not you, I bet.'

'Nobody's perfect.' He hefted his bedroll under one arm and his saddle under the other.

Silas Martin opened the door for him from the outside, the tiny gun back in its concealed holster. The sounds of the depot's bustle flowed into the shack on a stream of fresh, ice cold air. The stink of the injured men's bodies and clothing was immediately neutralised. Then the dampness of steam and the acrid taint of woodsmoke became prominent.

'The one with the beard I can understand,' Martin said, showing shock now, as he and the half-breed began crossing the tracks. 'He would have killed you for sure. But the old man . . .' He shook his head. '. . . The way you snapped his arm like it was a dead match. I think that's the most cold-blooded thing I ever did see.'

'Nobody asked you to watch, feller,' the glinting eyed half-breed replied.

'All he wanted was a drink.'

'The both of them did. Now they're a little smashed. Least they didn't die from thirst.'

CHAPTER FOUR

THE train with the crated coffin aboard was not the first to leave the depot. Instead, the two passenger trains were despatched with an hour separating their departures. Then the freight train made up of heavily laden flatcars. And it was close to five o'clock, when the sky was growing dark with evening, by the time the big locomotive at the head of the line of boxcars spun its wheels on the track, gained traction and finally inched into straining motion. Hauling more freight than originally intended because of a belated decision that two carloads of army supplies should be shipped to Fort Leavenworth.

With each train that pulled out of Denver the noise around the depot grew less and the bustle subsided.

Throughout the busy afternoon during which the temperature never rose above freezing, Edge stayed in or close to the boxcar containing the crate he was hired to guard. Silas Martin had kept him silent company at first, until they received news of the re-scheduling of train departures when the red faced old man had returned to the warmth of the main depot building. Twice he had brought out steaming mugs of coffee and handed them to Edge with the query:

'Everything's all right?'

The half-breed had replied with: 'Thanks. Sure.'

Neither man was happy about the delay and their disgruntlement was shared by everyone else anxious for the boxcar train to leave. The engineer, fireman and brakeman. A sergeant and five constables assigned by Chief Sorrel to guard against another attempt on Martin's crate while it was still within Denver city limits. And a bunch of ten hobos who had made some kind of deal with the brakeman to come aboard the train.

32

The crewmen kept to themselves on the locomotive foot-plate, warmed by the heat from the firebox.

The police officers were in the bitterly cold open, on the ground or rooftops, stratigically positioned to watch for the return of the surviving Japanese and to spring a trap if they appeared. But as the afternoon wore into evening they spent more and more time directing hostile stares toward the boxcar guarded by Edge. Whether their disgust was aimed at the half-breed or the crate over which he stood sentry, it was impossible to tell: only that they needed to blame somebody or something for the long and boring duty they had drawn.

It was not so difficult for the half-breed to reach a decision about the hobos, who had gathered in the shack with the shattered window and kept the stove alight against the bite of the intense cold. For he had watched them enter the frame building in ones and twos, and not seen Clyde and the old timer come out. The only person to emerge was the brakeman, after spending a few minutes inside, presumably taking up a collection which would render him temporarily blind as the train pulled out of the depot. Following this visit, the door of the shack remained firmly closed but at various times a series of heads showed at the smashed window: heads studded with embittered eyes in filthy and unshaven faces — aiming hate filled stares at the open door of the boxcar or the man who casually patrolled the track beside it.

The half-breed saw and noted everything of consequence without appearing to show interest in any of it. Which was the same impression of indifference he gave when two enclosed wagons rolled into the depot, each manned by four uniformed soldiers. The depot manager, looking more harassed than ever, superintended the transfer of more than sixty small wooden crates from the wagons to the two boxcars immediately in back of the one containing the corpse of Mrs Silas Martin.

Then, as soon as the transfer of freight was completed, the manager signalled the locomotive crew through the gathering murk of the Denver evening and the engineer gave a long blast on his steam whistle.

Edge thrust his Winchester into the car and hauled himself aboard.

Martin hurried out of the main building and made fast time in his waddling run to come around the rear of the caboose and along the side of the train. The spinning wheels of the locomotive had gained a grip on the track by then and the train was moving. So that the half-breed had to reach down and help the elderly, plump, red faced man aboard.

The brakeman had used some pretext to get the depot manager on the other side of the moving train. While the crewmen on the footplate peered ahead, eager to set their locomotive racing downhill toward the mid-western plains country.

So that only Edge and a half dozen Denver police officers saw the bunch of hobos break from the shack and advance on the train. Six of them making fast time while four straggled — two of them injured and the other two helping the casualties.

The lawmen cared nothing, merely grateful that the stint of boring and uncomfortable duty at the Union Pacific depot was over.

The half-breed remained at the open door of the boxcar for long enough to see all the unauthorised passengers get aboard: Clyde and the old-timer screaming their pain against the hiss of steam and clatter of wheels over switchgear as they were jerked roughly up off the ties and bundled into the boxcar. The third one back from where Edge banged the door closed and slid down it, sitting on his saddle.

'Any of Sorrel's men aboard?' Martin asked from where he sat on the floor of the car, leaning his back against the crate.

'You lost confidence in me already, feller?' the half-breed asked through the near complete darkness.

'No, certainly not. But I've been thinking. I've hired some help. So could Hitoshi. Unless the Denver police arrest him and Zenko first.'

'The two Japanese who rode out of the depot?'

'Yes. The one you killed was Toru. I presume you would like to hear about them? And why they are prepared to risk their lives to steal the body of my wife?'

34

'Why not? It's a long way to New York, feller. And you're the kind that has to talk about something.'

'Just that?' Martin sounded surprised. 'It doesn't intrigue you, what has happened? How do you know it is not me rather than the Japanese who is the wrongdoer? Or don't you care?'

Edge sighed. 'If I cared I know the Denver law is on our side. Even though we aren't exactly Sorrel's favourite people.'

'Of course. I now know you are the kind of man who does not need to hear the obvious stated.'

'But I figure I will,' the half-breed drawled. 'Seeing as how you're the kind of man who likes to talk. And that kind gets to repeat himself a lot of the time.'

The locomotive had strained to a steady speed and was now maintaining it easily, the wheels of the cars rolling smoothly over rails that curved gently to the left and then the right on a down grade. The lights of Denver were hidden on the high ground receding by the moment behind the caboose and full night had clamped down over the Colorado mountain country. But a near full moon hung against the star pricked blackness of the northern sky, its light augmented by reflection off the white snow that blanketed the rugged terrain to either side of the meandering track.

Some of this light trickled into the boxcar through the cracks surrounding the sliding doors on both sides. So Edge was able now to see the dark bulk of the crate containing the casket: and the moving form of the short, elderly Silas Martin as the man rose and began to prowl the car. Bitterly cold, frosty air also entered through the cracks and both men turned up their collars and hunched deeper into their coats.

'I may not look it, Mr Edge, but I come from a wealthy family. The Martins of Syracuse in western New York state.'

'Lots of people don't look what they are.'

'That's right. But I am not myself a man of means. I'm what is known as the black sheep of my family. I wasn't until late middle age. To the age of fifty-six I was a dutiful son, undertaking my appointed role as a vice-president in the Martin chain of shoe stores. You may have heard of us. We have stores in most of the large eastern cities?'

'Only time I was in the east I wasn't doing any shopping, feller. There was a war on.'

Martin pumped his head up and down vigorously. 'Of course. I understand. Anyway, at age fifty-six I was bitten by the wonderlust bug. No reason for it, except years and years of boredom. Even the war never touched me. Or perhaps it did, although not physically. Perhaps I was affected by the upheaval it caused. Anyway, I simply decided to leave, and leave I did. Travelled across country by train and boarded a China clipper in San Franscisco. Landed on a small island called Miyake off the east coast of Honshu. I don't suppose you know the area?'

'You don't suppose right,' Edge supplied.

'Sorry, I'm boring you?'

'If it gets too bad, I'll just go to sleep, feller.'

Martin believed this, and began to speak faster. 'Anyway it was only supposed to have been a stopover for me. But I ended up living on Miyake for more than eleven years. Raising rice, would you believe? Me, a glorified shoe clerk.' Now he shook his head. 'And I married. A beautiful girl young enough to be my grand-daughter, called Mai Lin. It was an idyllic life, Mr Edge. A beautiful island with a beautiful climate and shared with a beautiful young girl.

'But there was disease there and Mai Lin was struck down. A terrible disease because it is incurable. But mercifully the time between infection and death is short. One day Mai Lin was alive and healthy. Forty-eight hours later she was dead.'

Although there was no joy in the old man's tone, it was obvious that he relished telling this part of his story as much as he did talking about any other subject. He continued to pace up and down the smoothly rolling car, hands thrust deep into the pockets of his heavy, ankle length topcoat: like a schoolmaster lecturing on a topic dear to his heart.

Edge blew warm breath into hands cupped around his mouth.

'Because I knew the end was inevitable, I used those forty-eight hours to consider what I should do,' Martin went on, his own breath turning to white vapour the moment it was expelled from his lips. 'And I decided that I would bring the remains of Mai Lin home. To be interred in the Martin family vault at Syracuse.

'But it was easier thought about than done, Mr Edge. For Mai Lin was no ordinary Miyake girl. She was royalty. A kind of princess. And out there in the Pacific islands people of her bloodline are virtually religious beings.'

'Which was how you got to be such a good rice farmer, I guess?' Edge put in wryly.

'What?' The old man seemed to resent the interruption to his flow.

'You didn't just get one of the best women? She came complete with a piece of the best land.'

'No, that is not so!' came the fast response, the words hot with anger. 'There was no dowry. In life, Mai Lin's royal status was negligible. Women in the islands are very much second class citizens. Little more than servants and child-bearers. And their ancestry makes no difference to this.'

'Can see why you stayed, feller.'

Martin had to pace the whole length of the car before he recovered from the resentment and was able to pick up the thread of his story.

'It is only when a woman related to the emperor dies that her lineage becomes important. Because local lore dictates she has to be buried in the royal mausoleum. And I found that disgusting, Mr Edge. That the local people treated Mai Lin like so much dirt while she was alive and then were ready to go down on their knees and worship her when she was dead. And the best way I could think to show my feelings was to bring her body to this country. Which is what I did, with the help of another American who lives on Miyake. He had a small sailboat and he took me and the body to Honshu where I had the corpse embalmed and a lead lined casket made and crated. Then I shipped back to the United States aboard a

37

clipper bound for Portland, Oregon. I would have preferred San Francisco but I knew I was being followed by Samurai warriors and took passage on the first ship to leave Yokohama.'

'Who's Sam Urai?' Edge asked.

Silas Martin shook his head as he ceased his pacing and levered himself up to sit on the crate. He was not contemptuous of the half-breed's ignorance.

'Not who. What. Samurai are a Japanese fighting force. Toru was such a soldier. As are Hitoshi and Zenko. In the service of the emperor. Charged with retrieving the body of Mai Lin and returning it to be interred on the island of Miyake.' He sighed. 'I knew such men would be sent after me but I hadn't realised they were so close until I saw them at the railroad depot.'

He peered through the near darkness at Edge. The meagre moonlight shone on his silvery side-whiskers but did not illuminate the expression on his fleshy features. His tone betrayed weariness. 'I hired the Denver security men as a matter of course while we were snowed in. I'm afraid they did not believe my story and told the police. I was ordered to reveal the contents of the casket. And I'll do so again if you insist, Mr Edge. Although I would prefer not to. Several months have passed since poor Mai Lin was embalmed and . . .'

'She smells worse than your story,' the half-breed cut in.

'Then you do not believe me?' the tired old man responded, anxiety giving vigour to his tone.

'It sounds like bullshit and bullshit stinks, feller,' Edge said evenly.

'And so?'

'And so I didn't question you. You gave me answers which I don't have to like. We got a lot of miles to travel but I've already taken my pick. I don't want to open the box. I'll just have the money.'

'Now?'

'On delivery.'

'That seems fair, but I'd feel better if you accepted my word.'

The half-breed made no answer and a vocal silence settled inside the cold, dimly moonlit boxcar. The sounds of the train's progress down from the mountains continued to be regular: the click of wheels over expansion joints in the rails, the clatter of the bogies and the creaks of timber as the cars leaned toward the outside of the curves.

After a while, the noise began to have a soporific effect on the troubled mind of Silas Martin. His head dropped slowly forward so that his chin rested on his chest. He actually went to sleep sitting up for a few moments on a short stretch of straightaway. Then was jolted awake as the train took another curve and he started to topple.

'Do you mind if I bed down?' he asked.

'No sweat.'

His baggage had been aboard the car before the crate was loaded. It consisted of a large sea trunk and a carpetbag stacked in one corner. From the trunk he took three blankets and arranged them on top of the crate: one to lay on, one to cover himself and one which he rolled up as a pillow. He took off only his black derby before he slipped between the blankets and allowed the motion and sound of the train to lull him back into sleep.

It occurred briefly to Edge that the old man had elected to sleep on the crate for a particular reason: to prevent his new employee from reneguing on what he had said and taking a look inside.

But the narrow-eyed, thin-lipped man sitting easily on his saddle against the door felt no desire to check out Martin's story. All he cared about was that he was on the move again and that his journey had a purpose.

Snowbound Denver had been easy to take for awhile, as he rested up after the long cattle drive north and the period of self-doubt in Wyoming and during the ride south. But then the urge to hit the open trail had begun to irk him. Which was why he had hired out to help shovel snow from the Union Pacific depot: reasoning that the railroad would open for traffic ahead of the trails.

He had not needed the money he was paid, just as he did not need the job Silas Martin offered him for financial reward. For the cattle drive from the Rio Grande to Laramie had provided him with a good stake. What he did require was an aim. Increasingly of late he had discovered this. Money for food, liquor, tobacco and the other essentials of his kind of life was no longer enough.

And the initially strange events in the Wind River Range — which later turned out to be mundane — had driven home this fact. The fact that, having accepted he would never be allowed to fulfil his own selfish desires, the reason for his existence was to aid others whose destinies were ruled by a less cruel fate.

As his mind ranged over fresh memories of coincidental happenings in the Wyoming snow of Christmas, he absently drew the razor from the neck pouch and turned it slightly this way and that, so that its blade caught stray shafts of moonlight and glinted.

For once in the many years since he had taken the razor off a man in a Washington saloon during the bloody days of war, it had been put to a use that was good. When, in the hands of a doctor, it had made a cut which gave life to a new born baby.

The baby was not Jesus Christ come again and for this the mother and father were probably still giving thanks to God. Others had died — for nothing. But that was the way the breaks fell.

Edge could only follow his instincts, siding — for reward or not — with the faction that offered him the better chance of survival. And if his instincts steered him wrong? He could try to make amends. Like killing quickly a priest and a whore before they suffered too much on the brutal nails of crucifixion.

Who had been fulfilled then?

He grimaced through the darkness and pushed the razor back into the pouch. He was thinking the same brand of bullshit as Silas Martin had been talking. He was alive, with money in his pocket and he was on the move. That was all he gave a damn about. And he was allied with the old man because the old man was the one who had offered him a job. If the Samurai had been the first to put up money, he would probably have been with them: figuring out a way to steal the crated corpse.

He got to his feet, the familiar impassiveness taking over the lines of his lean face. His intention was simply to stretch his legs and flex the numbness of cold and inactivity out of his muscles. But a subdued thud on the roof of the car caused him to forego exercise simply for the sake of it. He stopped, slid the Winchester out of the saddleboot, and reached the side of the crate in two strides.

As he did this, three other thuds sounded through the more strident noise of the train's progress. He leaned down so that his face was only two inches above that of Silas Martin: and clamped a brown skinned hand over the old man's slightly parted lips. The sleeping man was jerked into terrified waking, his eyes snapping open: bulging to such an extent that they seemed in danger of popping out of their sockets.

'Easy,' the half-breed whispered. 'We've got company.'

The enlarged eyes travelled to their limit on either side. Then stared up at the roof as Edge made a gesture with his head and lifted his gagging hand.

'Best you get over in the corner behind your trunk, feller.'

Martin nodded his understanding. 'Zenko and Hitoshi?' he rasped as he slid out from under the blanket and began to unfasten his coat buttons.

'Four,' Edge replied, head cocked to listen for more sounds of movement on the roof of the car. 'And I figure they're more interested in the living than the dead.'

The old man delved a hand into his topcoat and under the lapel of his suit jacket. He pulled out a small, seven inch My Friend revolver with a ring grip.

'I bought it on Larimer Street three weeks ago,' he said when Edge glanced at the .32 calibre, five-shot gun. 'I've had some practice with it.'

'They say it makes perfect,' the half-breed rasped, gesturing for the old man to take up his position behind the sea trunk.

41

He went to the diagonally opposite corner of the car: certain that no others had joined the four men on the roof but unable to hear sounds of further movement. Not that it mattered. For the only means of access was through the sliding doors on either side and Edge and Silas Martin were each in a position to cover one of these.

The one on the right, which was covered by the old man, had never been fastened. The bolt screeching out of the bracket to free the opposite door gave the men inside advance warning that the intruders were poised to attack. Maybe as much as a complete second. Then the doors shrieked along their metal runners. Bitingly cold air whooshed into the car. Stark white, moonlighted mountainscape flashed by. Blurred by speed.

Patches of a brighter, yellow light showed at the tops of the doorways.

'For Clyde!' a man roared.

'And Benny!' Another man at the other door.

The words heard then snatched away by the slipstream of the train roaring into another curve.

The patches of bright light went from sight, then arced down below the level of the roof.

Edge fired the Winchester from the hip and for an instant the area of yellow light doubled in size: to the sound of shattered glass as his bullet smashed into the swinging kerosene lamp.

Then a man screamed as flaming oil was sprayed against his flesh, hair and clothing.

Martin's tiny gun cracked, the bullet tunnelling uselessly through the frosty air outside.

The second lamp remained intact until it hit the crate and bounced to the floor of the car: to spread fiercely burning oil in every direction.

'Jesus!' the old man wailed.

'Use the blankets!' Edge yelled at him as he lunged away from the corner, angling the rifle upward.

With both doors open the sounds of the train's downhill

motion were stridently loud. The burning man was still screaming. The air-fanned flames inside the car roared greedily.

The half-breed blasted shots at the roof. Chips of timber rained down as the bullets punched holes to admit tiny shafts of moonlight.

With curses ripping from his trembling lips, Silas Martin raced to the crate, grabbed a blanket in each hand and began to beat at the fire.

Edge uttered no sound as he pumped the lever action of the rifle and squeezed the trigger. Five times in all. No human voice rose above the roar and clatter to indicate that any of the bullets had hit an unseen target. The burning man was no longer screaming his searing agony.

Martin began to win against the fire, his curses choked off as the billowing smoke was sucked into his lungs. He was in a frantic world of his own as he raised each arm in turn and brought the blanket flailing down on the flames. So that he vented a gasp of alarm when the half-breed leaned close to yell in his ear:

'Give me a hand, feller!'

This said, Edge moved to the crate and started to push against it. The old man hesitated only a moment, then abandoned his fire-fighting to add his weight and strength to that of the half-breed. Suddenly he was struck by a fearful thought.

'You're not going to...'

But Edge straightened up before the crate was in danger of tipping out of the car.

'No, I'm not,' he answered, snatching up the Winchester and climbing on the crate.

The area of flames had spread on the car floor and Martin grabbed the blankets and started to beat at them again.

Edge hooked one hand over the side of the roof as his hat was whipped off his head, the thong cutting into his neck. His long hair blew across his eyes but he was still able to see through the waving strands.

Two men lay on the flat roof of the boxcar, held by the total inertia of death. One had a hole in his cheek which had

43

spilled a pool of blood that was beginning to freeze. The other was hairless and almost naked, his exposed flesh charred matt black by the fierce flames which had killed him.

The two survivors were on the roof of the car behind, moving with a splayed leg gait and arms out to the sides as they balanced on the swaying surface. They had their backs to Edge and did not dare check behind them for fear that such a move might upset their equilibrium and send them toppling over the side.

Edge had ample time to lodge the rifle safely under the weight of the nearest corpse and then to use both arms to haul himself up on to the roof. Then to sprawl out prone and, with the unburned body as a rest, take aim along the car roofs.

It needed only one shot, fired by a man who did not have to consider for a moment the morality of what he was doing.

Two men had attempted to steal from him and he had punished them. That should have been the end of it. But the law of the hobo jungle did not accept this. So friends of the injured men had tried to reap revenge on their behalf. Their failure had cost them two lives and their only weapons. Edge had survived, still in possession of the means to assuage his own desire for vengeance.

This is how his thoughts would have run had he applied his mind to the subject. Instead, he simply muttered: 'Meet fire with fire,' and squeezed the Winchester's trigger.

The hobo in the lead was crouched to leap from one car to the next. Edge's bullet drilled into the back and smashed the spine of the second man. Who arched his body and was driven forward — to slam into the first one.

There was just a single scream: short-lived, as both men were pitched down between the cars: to bounce off the couplings and be cut in half by the first set of wheels to make contact with their flesh.

'They coming back?' Silas Martin shrieked fearfully.

'Maybe there's a ghost of a chance,' the half-breed muttered.

CHAPTER FIVE

HE ROLLED over on to his back and turned around: to use his feet to push the two bodies off the roof. The thuds of dead weight hitting snow at the trackside were masked by the much louder sounds of the speeding train.

'Edge?' Martin yelled, the terror of being left alone sending his voice to a falsetto pitch.

'Relax, feller!' the half-breed called.

'Thank God,' the old man rasped, then raised his voice: 'The fire's out!'

'Heat's off here, too. For awhile.'

But the blazing cord wood in the locomotive's firebox continued to bellow smoke up and out of the balloon smokestack and, as the rails came out of a curve at the start of a straightaway, the acrid black vapour began to stream along the car roofs and envelope the half-breed.

Holding his breath behind lips clamped tightly closed, he crawled to the rear of the roof and climbed carefully down the iron rungs of the ladder. Outside, clinging precariously with one hand to the cold metal, the swaying motion of the car seemed to be emphasised.

The coupling was of the link-and-pin type and Edge allowed himself a low grunt of satisfaction when he saw this. Then he dismissed all futile thoughts from his mind as he swung from the ladder to place a foot firmly on the tail drawbar of one car and the front bar of the next. Beneath his splayed legs the neatly aligned ties rushed by in a blurring optical illusion which made them appear to be formed into one continuous length of timber.

With his right shoulder braced against the rear of the boxcar carrying the crate, he worked the lever action of the Winchester. And rested the muzzle against one side of the link as he squeezed the trigger.

The report was deafeningly loud between the walls of the cars. The bullet bit into the metal and ricocheted. The recoil jolted him from fingertips to shoulders.

Another futile thought tried to enter his mind: of the certain death that would come to him if he fell on to the track. He had to make an effort to drive it from him. The fear which expanded from the pit of his stomach to engulf his entire body was colder than the air whipping in around the trailing corners of the leading car. Hot beads of sweat pumped from his pores and immediately became icy on his flesh.

A spot of silver showed on the link and he rested the rifle muzzle on this to explode another shot. Six times he fired at the metal and on each occasion he endured the sweating fear of sudden, bloody death. But his well developed muscles held him balanced and none of the ricochets came close to spinning into his legs.

The expanse of silver metal grew over the grease blackened link. But the coupling held firm until, gripping a ladder rung again, the half-breed began to stamp on the bullet weakened iron. When it snapped, he made no vocal sound. Simply worked saliva into his fear parched mouth and spat it down at the track.

The train was still steaming down the grades of the Continental Divide's eastern slopes, so there was little strain on the fractured link. And the line of boxcars was still strung together when Edge tossed his empty rifle in through the doorway and then lowered himself from the roof and swung in its wake.

An anxious, strangely white-faced Silas Martin demanded: 'What on earth has been going on out there?'

Not until he was in the partial shelter of the car, with both doors still open to the night, did the half-breed realise how cold he was. Before he even acknowledged that he had heard the question, he dragged both doors closed, shutting out most of the icy draughts and a lot of the noise. Then he sat down and hung his own two blankets over his shoulder. He had to blow into his cupped hands for more than half a minute before his fingers were flexible enough to take shells from his pocket and feed them through the loading gate of the Winchester. The smell of burnt timber was very strong, but less cloying than the stench of charred flesh which had briefly assaulted his nostrils on the roof.

'Four gone, six to go,' he said.

'What?'

'Hobos, feller. When we reach level ground or start on an upgrade, this car'll be the caboose.'

'There are more of them ready to try to kill us?'

'There are more of them,' Edge answered evenly. 'The old timer and the red haired feller ain't in any condition to make it over the roofs. Figured it best not to take a chance on the other four.'

Still bitterly cold, but no longer having to keep his teeth clenched to stop them from chattering, the half-breed got stiffly to his feet and slid open the door: far enough to push his head through. He looked forward first, and the thong cut into his throat again as his hat was blown off. His lips curled back from his teeth when he saw that the downgrade ended at the start of a long trestle bridge a half mile away. A river, swollen and fast flowing with melted snow, rushed angrily around the bridge supports far below. On the far side the ground rose, the railroad curving gently to left and right again to minimise the effect of the grade.

When he turned his attention toward the second half of the train, two heads were quickly withdrawn into the car carrying the hobos. Then Edge pulled back out of the slipstream, his mirthless grin broadening.

Silas Martin was sitting on the crate, wrapped in two charred blankets and an undamaged one. Anxiety continued to cut deep lines into his pale, waxy face smudged with soot on the forehead. The danger and exertion of putting out the fire had weakened him and he looked much older.

'You enjoy killing, don't you?' he asked.

47

Edge leaned against the partially open door. 'I enjoy staying alive, feller,' he corrected. 'Lot of the time it works out I have to kill to stay alive. So I guess maybe you could say I enjoy killing.'

'I'm not criticising, you understand. As far as the men who attacked us are concerned. But the others? And the brakeman will be left behind, too. They could die of exposure out here in the mountains.'

'Or they could be picked up by the next train through, feller. The brakeman let the hobos aboard.'

Martin shrugged. 'I don't know.' He sighed. 'All I do know is that I'd feel better about all of them if they had been intent on stealing Mai Lin's body.'

The sounds of the train's progress altered tone as the wheels rolled on to track stretching out over the trestle bridge.

'You value that more than your life?' Edge growled.

'Of course not. But it just seems to me you are too free with other people's lives.'

'Not free, feller,' the half-breed responded as he turned toward the gap in the door again. 'On this job I come at five dollars a day.'

Air rushed around his head and billowed his long hair. The boxcar was halfway across the bridge and the broken link of the coupling continued to hold. Then the note of the locomotive's roar altered in pitch as it started up the grade, the pistons and drive shafts protesting at the extra strain.

The engineer held his throttle full open as the fireman stoked greater heat under the boiler. The speed dropped noticeably but the drive wheels maintained their traction on the sloping rails. One by one the string of cars were hauled off the wooden bridge and up the incline.

The coupling held.

Edge waited and watched and experienced a moment of doubt when the caboose started uphill, adding its weight to that of five boxcars pulling against the broken link. But then he snatched a look forward and pursed his lips. There was something like a mile of switch-backing track to the crest of the rise, which allowed ample time and distance for his plan to take effect.

It happened less than a minute later, as the train snaked out of a left hand curve to take a right. The link sprang open with a creak of tortured metal, then snapped cleanly where it hooked around the pin.

The locomotive, relieved of better than half its payload, lunged into a spurt of acceleration. The freed cars rolled a few feet under forward momentum, then halted briefly and started to move in reverse: gaining speed with every foot of downgrade they covered.

Metal screeched on metal as the engineer and brakeman realised that something was badly wrong. The locomotive, already fighting the upgrade, came to a shuddering, steam-hissing halt in less than fifty feet.

Edge remained sure footed, braced against the partially open door. But Silas Martin was hurled painfully to the floor when the car thudded hard against the one ahead.

In the caboose, the brakeman worked frantically at his wheel: locking and then releasing the blocks which spat showers of sparks across the track each time they touched the rims. But the free-wheeling cars were thrusting too hard, bringing to bear every ounce of their freight's weight. So that even when the brakes locked the wheels, the speed of the runaway string of cars did not slacken.

From the locomotive cabin, the engineer and fireman stared in horror. Silas Martin forced the door wider to stand beside Edge and began to shake his head and clench and unclench his fists.

The half-breed muttered: 'Stupid sonofabitch.'

The runaway cars had thundered around the bend, their wheels maintaining a grip on the rails. The caboose started out across the straight, level bridge, pushed to an even higher speed by the final thrust of the heavily laden cars still on the slope. Heads showed at the doorway of the car carrying the hobos. The distance was too great for their expressions to be seen: but the four watchers aboard the stalled section of the train could sense terror, like a palpable presence, emanating from the car.

The last spurt of speed triggered panic in the minds of everyone riding the runaway cars. And the lone railman, who should have known better, surrendered to an impulse.

Had he waited for a few more seconds he would have felt the momentum ease as all the cars attained the level top of the bridge. But the brakeman went for broke too soon: spinning the wheel and leaning hard across it to force the blocks against the rims and lock the wheels.

Steam hissed furiously through the safety valves of the locomotive's boilers: filling the snow blanketed valley with its sound. So that, for a long time the destruction of half a train seemed — to the quartet of watchers — to happen without noise.

The caboose came to a halt for part of a second. Then all five cars slammed into each other, their wheels jumping the rails. Two went to the left and two to the right. The caboose simply crumpled. The apex of the 'V' formed by the jack-knifing cars reached out over the side of the unfenced bridge. And dipped down toward the white rushing water of the swollen river far below.

Because all sounds of the wreck were masked by hissing steam, the sight of the toppling cars took on an unreal quality to the watchers. The crash and fall seemed to happen too slowly: as if time had speeded up and was now correcting itself.

Two human forms slid from the hobos' boxcar, arms flailing and legs kicking — as if the doomed men were trying to swim in mid-air.

Then the entire nose-diving wreckage exploded: was enveloped in a massive ball of broiling red and blue flame. The slopes of the valley trembled under the blast as the deafening report assaulted the ears of the watchers.

Minor avalanches tipped snow down the steepest slopes.

The ball of fire broke up into a rain of flames pouring out of a cloud of oily black smoke. Slipstream put out the flames long

50

before charred pieces of the bridge, the cars and corpses plunged into the river.

Time slid by at its normal rate. The cold mountain air neutralised the stench of burning. Eardrums recovered from the shockwave of the blast. Moving snow halted and piled up.

'Friction, I guess!' a man said, shouting hoarsely above the hiss of steam. 'Must have been explosives in those army supplies! Friction and a spark!'

Edge shifted his narrow-eyed gaze away from the fire blackened gap at the top of the trestle bridge: to look down at the oil-smeared face of the tubby engineer. The man was breathless, with shock and the exertion of running down the sides of the train from his locomotive.

'Guess so,' the half-breed agreed.

The engineer went to check on the drawbar at the rear of the car.

Martin began to glare hatefully at Edge, but brought his feelings under control when he met the glinting-eyed stare of the taller man.

'Damn this penny-pinchin' railroad for not using the knuckle couplers!' the engineer snarled as he returned to the side of the car. 'Link must have snapped like a dry twig!' He gazed ruefully down at the yawning gap in the bridge, then struck an open palm with a fist. 'And damn Riley, too! If he'd have left the damn brakes alone the friggin' cars would have stopped safe as can be.' He shook his head in non-comprehension. 'Can't understand it! Riley was a long service brakeman!'

Edge shrugged his broad shoulders. 'Sometimes a feller ain't himself when he's at a loose end.'

CHAPTER SIX

THE SIGN on the Union Pacific building proclaimed: BUTCHERVILLE. Which suggested a town. But it was not. It was comprised of a single depot building, one storey high, with a water tower on the roof: sited at the end of a boardwalk beside the track. A quarter of a mile to the north there was the house, barn and corral of a small farmstead, huddled in back of snow-covered fields.

No lights showed against the darkness of the buildings as the train slowed for its approach to the water halt, which was situated on an otherwise featureless plain twenty miles east of the Rockies foothills. Even when the engineer gave a shrill blast on his whistle, the buildings continued to stand in solid blackness against the shallow, powdery snow.

The high pitch blast of sound roused Edge and Silas Martin from sleep: the half-breed instinctively taking a firmer grip on the frame of his Winchester while the old man delved a hand under his coat.

'We're slowing down!' Martin croaked anxiously.

'You worry too much, feller,' the half-breed growled.

While the old man remained in a tense, sitting up attitude atop the crated casket, Edge got to his feet, slid open the nearest door and looked along the length of the train. After looking briefly at the tiny depot, he checked the view from the other door and saw the farmstead.

'What's the trouble?' the old man demanded as Edge returned to the door on the depot side of the car.

'Maybe none, if the feller who runs this water stop is hard of hearing.'

The engineer brought his locomotive to a halt alongside the depot building and vented another shrill whistle into the early hours. The sound caused a spasm of trembling to grip Martin, but the old man controlled it as he slid off the crate, shrugging out of the blankets.

'Stay aboard,' Edge instructed as he dropped down on to the lightly snow-covered boardwalk. 'And keep your eyes on the farm over there. You see anything you don't like, come running. Okay?'

The old man nodded. 'Sure.' But he didn't look sure of anything.

The half-breed started along toward the depot building, where the engineer and fireman were thudding fists against a one piece wooden door. As he went by the gaps between the cars, he glanced across the fields at the farmhouse. It remained in darkness. The even surface of the snow covering the fields has been disturbed by booted feet criss-crossing between the farm and the depot.

'Nobody home?' Edge asked.

'Where the frig would Dave go?' the lanky young fireman snapped, then winced as the engineer rapped him on the shin with a boot cap.

The fireman's ill temper vanished when he turned to look into the flint-eyed gaze of the half-breed: who he had seen shoot down two men at the Denver depot.

Edge kept his tone even, guessing that there had been a great deal of talk about him in the cabin of the locomotive. 'Farmhouse across the way?' he suggested.

'I guess he visits,' the engineer allowed. 'But not close to train times.'

'You need him to take on water? Can't you handle it your-selves?'

The fireman shook his head. 'Ain't water we need Dave for. Phil here says the telegraph line across the bridge still looked to be in some kind of shape after the explosion, mister. We gotta try to wire Denver about the bridge gettin' knocked out.'

'Guess you have,' Edge acknowledged, leaned forward, turned the handle and swung the door open.

'Damnit, why didn't we think of that!' the fireman growled.

53

'On account of us havin' other things on our minds,' the engineer answered.

He followed his crewman into the building and seemed nervous at having the rifle-carrying half-breed behind him.

The windows were shuttered, but enough moonlight came in through the open door to show the shadowy forms of the furnishings. The lanky fireman struck a match to light a kerosene lamp. The yellow glow illuminated an immaculately neat and tidy office with timetables and paintings of railroad scenes hung on the walls. There was a desk in the centre of the room with a padded chair behind it. Against a wall was a table with a wooden chair pushed under it. On the table was telegraph equipment, a pile of wire blanks and a spike heavy with used message sheets. A pot-bellied stove in a corner was cold and smelled of dead ashes.

The dead body in the combination kitchen and bedroom at the rear of the building had not started to smell. Edge saw it first, as merely a dark hump in crumpled human form on the floor between the end of the narrow bed and the cooking range.

'That Dave?' he asked, stepping to the side of the doorway so that the fireman could reach over the threshold with the lamp.

'God, yes!' the lanky young man gasped.

Phil peered between the two taller men and made a choking sound deep in his throat. But he backed away and was able to contain the vomit in his stomach.

The Union Pacific's man in Butcherville had died of a stab wound in the throat. He was still alive when he hit the floor and had lived for a few moments longer. Pain or the terror of drowning on his own arterial blood had caused him to thrash around on the floor. Blood, black now from exposure to the cold air, was spread on the boarding to either side of him and was crusted on his shirt front and his hands.

'What's happening?' the pale-faced Silas Martin called from the boardwalk.

'The despatcher's been despatched,' Edge growled, whirling

and striding across the neat office. 'You ain't supposed to be here.'

'The house looks deserted. You were so long and it was so quiet. I got nervous.'

'Hey!' Phil called as the half-breed stepped outside.

'Do something for you, feller?'

'Either of you know how to work a telegraph key?'

'You work it up and down,' Edge answered.

The engineer scowled.

'Maybe there's a book around. But I'd check the connection first.'

The short, tubby man seemed to be rooted to the spot by the shock of finding the body. And it was the fireman who went to the table and stooped over the equipment.

'Phil?'

'Yeah, Ollie?'

'He's right. It ain't just Dave that's dead.'

As the heat from the unstoked flames in the locomotive's firebox grew less, so the sound of steam hissing from the safety valve dropped in volume. Silence crowded in off the plain.

'Ollie?'

'Yeah, Phil?'

'I think we should get the hell outta here.'

'We gotta take on water or end up stranded in the friggin' middle of nowhere.'

'So fill her up.'

Both men stepped out on to the boardwalk and came to an abrupt halt. Silas Martin was standing with his back to the tender, swinging the My Friend revolver from side to side to cover the engineer and fireman.

'You're to do what you have to do, gentlemen,' he said, confident of his ability to stand guard over two unarmed railroad men. 'In order to make the train ready to leave. But we won't depart until Mr Edge returns.'

The engineer was still suffering from shock and he was

afraid of the swinging gun. But the absence of Edge enabled the fireman to give free rein to his temper again.

'Frig off, you little runt,' he snarled. 'The way I see it the big guy is the reason for all the trouble we been havin'. So if he ain't back when we filled the tanks, it won't be no hardship headin' out without him! And remember, old timer. You blast Phil and me and won't no one leave Butcherville tonight! Unless you and the big guy can run a locomotive?'

Silas Martin's new found confidence drained out of him in face of the lanky young man's tirade. But Ollie made no move against him: simply spun into a half turn and strode toward the bracket which held the water hose fast to the front of the building.

'He ain't really like that, mister,' the nervous engineer explained. 'I guess he's as scared as I am. Sounds off like that to pretend he ain't.'

Martin nodded, his features expressing sympathy. 'I can understand that. I wouldn't normally hold a gun on innocent men. But I'm scared, too. And I'll tell you something.'

'What?'

'If you and he don't do exactly what my partner wants, I'm scared enough to kill the both of you.'

The engineer swallowed hard, certain that he was hearing the truth.

The fireman could hear only the low hiss of escaping steam and his own whispered curses as he climbed up on to the locomotive, dragging the hose toward the tank filler cap.

Edge was far enough away from the stalled train to be only vaguely aware of the sounds made by the locomotive. To his ears, his breathing was a louder noise.

After leaving the depot building he had stepped off the boardwalk on the other side from the train and remained erect as he moved — until he was level with the final boxcar which still had both doors gaping open. Then he went out full length and bellied over the frost crusted snow. At first the timber supports of the boardwalk and the deep shadows among them provided cover. Then, when this ran out, there were just the rails on the ties between him and the dark, silent farmstead.

He knew that, even flat to the white-covered, bitterly cold ground, he was not entirely hidden. That each time he slid himself forward another couple of feet, there was a possibility he would be seen — as a patch of moving darkness on immobile whiteness behind gleaming, inert rails. But nobody saw him, for nobody had a reason to look in the direction he was taking. As far as the watchers were concerned, all activity was centred upon the head of the halted train.

That there were watchers, Edge had no doubt: and he did not base this conviction on the war-taught ability to sense eyes directing their attention toward him. Instead, he reasoned that the killing of the Butcherville despatcher was not an isolated incidence of wanton violence: and chose to believe, until events proved otherwise, that the murder had a connection with the shootings at the Denver Union Pacific depot. A choice that arose out of his cynical philosophy that if a man constantly expected the worst of any situation, he could never be disappointed. Sometimes might be pleasantly surprised.

Some eighty feet behind the last boxcar he reached a position of relative safety: could rise on to all fours and crawl over the track to squat behind a four feet high bank. He used the barrel of the Winchester to check that the bank was composed of something more substantial than drifted snow and grunted his satisfaction when he discovered frozen earth beneath the sprinkling of crunchy whiteness.

Then he glanced back along the track at the depot for the first time since leaving it: and saw the fireman hosing water into the locomotive's tanks while Silas Martin continued to aim his small revolver at the engineer. The lanky fireman was a starkly moonlit figure atop the big engine. His partner and the old man were less distinct, in the shadow of the tender and silhouetted against the faint glow which escaped from the closed door of the firebox.

Then the half-breed shifted his narrow-eyed gaze back to the dark shapes of the farmhouse and barn, as he cocked the hammer of the Winchester and pressed the barrel down to make an indentation in the snow at the side of the bank. And now he did give free rein to his sixth sense for detecting the hostile presence of unseen watchers.

The hair at the nape of his neck felt prickly and there were beads of sweat on his palms where they curled tightly around the cold metal and wood of the rifle's frame and stock. But he set little store by these reactions, which was characteristic of him. Back on those eastern battlegrounds he had been young and inexperienced, filled with the hopes of youth and susceptible to the imaginings of a mind not yet brutalised by the harshness that was to come. Perhaps in those days, when death had quite literally lurked behind every bush or wall, his life had been saved by an uncanny perception for hidden danger.

Down the years, during the war and in its bloody aftermath, the realities of survival had allowed little scope for him to indulge himself in the vagaries of such variables as luck and allied abstract powers. But always in a situation such as this, when he was certain of his physical abilities and there was time to spare, he attempted to re-kindle that old sixth sense. Aware that he was getting into the realm of imagination and in the full knowledge that his hunches had been wrong more times than they had been right.

So he looked upon it simply as a mental exercise which kept his mind occupied — with thought processes of his own choosing. Which was better than having to struggle against the assault of a stream of thinking he had no wish to indulge.

'Hold it right there, trainman!' a voice boomed. 'Move and you'll be dead before you hit the ground!'

The warning was shouted from the farmhouse, the words reaching the depot distinctly across the quarter mile of snow-covered fields. The lanky fireman had filled both tanks of the locomotive and was about to swing down on to the boardwalk when the first word boomed out.

Edge glanced along the track and saw the man freeze. While below him the engineer and Silas Martin dropped to their haunches and shuffled forward and across to peer between the rear of the tender and front of the first boxcar.

'And if somebody else tries anythin', you'll be just as dead!'

The man was using something to amplify his voice. Maybe hands cupped around his mouth.

A cry sounded at the front of the train. Edge looked along the track and saw a muzzle flash: little more than a spark over such a distance. The crack of Martin's tiny revolver hardly sounded above the gentle hiss of escaping steam.

'Oliver!' the tubby engineer shrieked.

'Edge!' Silas Martin yelled, the voices of both men reaching to falsetto under the pressure of fear.

'I friggin' warned you!' the man at the house boomed and punctuated his enraged words with rifle shot.

But the fireman had started to move on Martin's shout — leaping down from the locomotive to thud his booted feet on the boardwalk close to where his partner and the old man were rolling frantically from side to side, locked in a clawing embrace.

The half-breed had shifted his glinting eyes back to the farmstead by then. And curled his thin lips away from his teeth to show a cruel grin as he heard angry voices and the stomping of fast moving feet on floor boarding. Then the snort of an ill-treated horse and the creak of unoiled door hinges.

The shot from the house sent a bullet thwacking into a timber strut supporting the water tower.

Silas Martin screamed and lay still.

Phil moaned: 'Oh my God!' and hurled away the damaging revolver.

His lanky partner hauled him up off the spread-eagled form of the bleeding old man and snarled: 'Let's get outta here!'

Two men rode out of the barn, ducking their heads to avoid the lintel. When they came erect the reins were gripped in their teeth, leaving their hands free to fire repeating rifles. The bullets they exploded clanged against the metal of the loco-

59

motive. Another man lunged from the doorway of the house, shouting incoherently as he loosed a volley of shots on the run.

The half-breed's evil grin had a fixed quality for part of a second: as the gunfire was all but lost amid a clamorous roar of power from the locomotive. He snapped another glance along the track and compressed his lips. Of the trio of men who had been on the boardwalk, only Silas Martin was still in sight: his unmoving form clear to see in the bright glow from the open firebox — before a great billow of steam broiled over him.

The drive wheels of the engine spun on the rails. Sand showered down. Rims bit the track and the thrusting power of the open throttle reached through the frantically working pistons to inch the locomotive into painfully slow movement. The line of boxcars shuddered and clanked out of inertia.

Edge struggled to quell the hot anger that threatened to engulf him, succeeded, and was surprised at having experienced the emotion. His tone was as ice cold as the snow beneath his prone body when he muttered: 'Cool it, feller.' And shot the running man.

In the chest, left of centre: the bullet stopping the man in his tracks and then causing him to corkscrew to the snow.

The two riders were far ahead of the man on foot, their attention concentrated on the locomotive as it picked up speed. The sounds of the moving train and the fusillade of shots from their own rifles masked the crack of Edge's Winchester.

The half-breed killed the rider nearest him with a bullet that drilled through the man's side, entering above the right hip bone on an upward trajectory, passing between two ribs and coming to rest buried deep in the heart. As the lead tunnelled through flesh the man had time to scream his agony and fling away his rifle. The sound was loud and shrill enough to reach the ears of his partner: who snapped his head around as the dying man pitched sideways off his mount.

'Bad things,' Edge rasped between teeth bared again in an evil grin, 'come in threes.'

It had to be a back shot because the half-breed did not trust himself to hit the smaller target of the screwed around head of the man. In the moonlight he saw the hole appear in the light coloured material of the rider's coat. Watched for a moment as the bloodstain blossomed larger. Then powered to his feet and lunged into a flat out run as his third victim fell forward, bounced against the neck of the horse and was hurled into just another pile of dead flesh on the snow.

Conscious that there might be more than three ambushers, Edge cast several glances toward the darkened farmstead as he sprinted alongside the track. But no muzzle flash showed to signal a shot.

He reached the western end of the depot boardwalk just as the final boxcar was hauled clear of the eastern end. The locomotive, not yet with a full head of steam but hauling only half its normal payload, was gaining speed with every yard of track it covered.

But the running half-breed was closing on his objective: and did not break his loping gait as he saw Silas Martin raise his head and heard him call: 'Edge!'

'Got a train to catch,' he gasped between quick breaths.

'Don't leave me!' the old man cried weakly as the half-breed raced by him.

Edge saw the blood on the front of Martin's coat, glimpsed the pleading look on the deathly pale features between the bushy sidewhiskers and experienced regret that he had no time to explain. Another uncharacteristic emotion. Compounded by a gesture.

He flung the Winchester across the track. It hit the side of the boardwalk and fell to the ties.

Then he was beyond the injured old man, starting to feel sharp pains across his chest at the unaccustomed exertion. His breathing became laboured. His eyes began to smart and blur. But he kept up the punishing pace, fighting the need to cough as locomotive smoke billowed around him. A drumming in his ears blotted out the sounds of the train. He started to feel light headed.

But by then he had drawn level with the rear of the final boxcar. He was gripped by a sensation of elation and felt he could leap forward and up to grasp the iron ladder.

He quelled the feeling and drove himself to a final burst of speed that placed himself alongside the open door. He reached up with one long arm, curled his fingers around the doorframe, almost stumbled, then powered upward and to the side, both legs continuing to pump as though his feet were still slamming at solid ground instead of thin air.

One booted foot hooked over the floor of the car while the other failed to make the height. His kneecap bumped over ties and he cursed at the pain, willing strength into his punished muscles. He heaved with one arm and one leg and a moment later was sprawled face down on the floor of the car. Sweat beads turned to pinpricks of ice on his flesh and the aches in his chest, legs and arms screamed for relief. When he squeezed his eyelids tight shut it seemed impossible to open them again.

Then the drumming against his ears took on a different note, changing in pitch and cadence. He had to listen to it for several moments before he realised that the sound came from outside his skull — was caused by the clatter of the car wheels. He snapped open his eyes and turned his head to the side. The snow-covered trackside began to blur as Phil and Ollie urged the locomotive faster.

His punished body protesting with a higher degree of pain, he rose on to all fours, crawled to the other side of the crate and pressed a shoulder to the unplaned timber. At his first attempt there was no movement. Then, urging himself to greater effort with curses rasped between clenched teeth, he tried again. It seemed to be another failure but then the crate containing the leadlined casket moved a fraction of an inch. And, with this small start made, he used the momentum to keep the slide going: altering his posture to use hands, shoulders and chest.

His eyes were closed again and the drumming inside his head blotted out the sounds of the speeding train. A rush of cold slipstream against his sweating face warned him he was close to the door. Then the crate tipped and he experienced the sweet relief of not having to push it any more. It went out of the car and he did not hear the clatter as it hit the ground: as he struggled to prevent himself following it before he was ready.

He desperately wanted to rest his aching body: even considered doing this and then working forward along the roofs of the boxcars to the locomotive.

But he jumped, suspecting the crew were aware he had boarded the train: not knowing if they carried weapons in the cabin — and concerned to get back to the injured Silas Martin as soon as he could.

The luck in which he did not believe but accepted in whatever form it came, was with him. His legs were bent and he spread his arms: ready to absorb the impact of landing and to retain his balance for as long as he could. But he came to a soft stop, his feet sinking deep into a pile of old snow drifted against some high brush — his body whip-lashing forward to slam into more cushioning whiteness.

The train rattled away from him and he coughed on the smoke it trailed. He closed his eyes again and swallowed the snow that melted in his mouth. His skull was filled with sounds he could not identify. When they had subsided, so had the noise of the speeding train. The white covered world was abruptly silent. Then he heard his own breathing. And the crunching of compacted snow as he moved — rolling over on to his back and sitting up.

There was not even the taint of woodsmoke in the bitingly cold air now. The stars against the blackness of the unclouded sky looked close enough to reach out and touch. The moonlight seemed much brighter.

He eased to his feet, wincing against the pains, which were at their sharpest down the long lengths of his legs. He blinked his eyes to clear the final blur of mistiness from his vision and looked back along the glinting rails.

The crate lay close to the track a hundred and fifty feet

away. More than half a mile beyond this was the dark bulk of the Butcherville depot building with the water tower atop it. Across the fields from this, the farmstead was still unlit. Three small, dark humps showed on the whiteness of the fields. All that moved back there were two horses, walking nervously over to where their riders lay.

Silas Martin was no longer sprawled on the boardwalk: was nowhere that the half-breed could see.

Far off, in the other direction, the rear of the train was a diminishing dot between the gleaming rails.

He flexed his muscles and moved tentatively out of the snowdrift, his tone sour as he muttered: 'I thought the train was supposed to take the strain.'

By the time he reached the crate, he was walking easier but he did not make the mistake of going down on to his haunches to examine the timber. The crate had hit the ground without the benefit of more than an inch of snow to cushion the impact, but it seemed to have survived without splitting open on three sides or either end.

As he continued, he was able to quicken his pace without too much discomfort and when he reached the eastern end of the boardwalk his pains had been reduced to dull aches.

'Act naturally, Mr Edge. It's not finished yet.'

Martin's voice was a weak whisper, trembling with nervousness.

'How many?' the half-breed asked, not moving his lips as came to a halt and eased his rump gratefully down on to the side of the boardwalk.

He had seen the old man, lying curled up on his side in the deep shadow under the boarding, both hands fisted tightly around the Winchester. Now, feigning a weariness it would have been simple to genuinely feel, he massaged his bristled cheeks and gazed across the fields at the farmstead.

'Only heard one. Couldn't get what he was saying. But he must have been talking to somebody else.'

'How badly you hurt, feller?'

64

'Bad enough. But I can hold out long enough to cover you. It's the obvious place you'd go. Over there.'

'If you have to, shoot as straight as you think, Silas,' Edge growled and pushed himself up from the boardwalk.

He stepped over the track and started across the fields, his chosen course of a straight line taking him between the two horses nuzzling their dead riders and meaning he had to lengthen his stride to pass over the body of the first of the ambushers he had killed. Not until he had done this did he raise his right hand to drape it on the butt of the holstered Remington.

'Now to the belt buckle, mister! Unhook it and let it fall.'

Edge halted but kept his hand where it was. His eyes, narrowed to the merest slivers of ice blueness, raked from the door to the window of the farmhouse and back again. The door was still open. With the moon behind the house, the window looked matt black. He was twenty feet from the front of the house. The barn was thirty feet to his right. A horse made soft noises inside the latter. The man who spoke out of the former sounded as nervous as Silas Martin a few minutes ago.

'You got a good reason to kill me, feller?' the half-breed asked evenly.

'Only one I need is iffen you don't do like I say.' As nervous and perhaps as old as Martin.

'You got a gun aimed at me?'

'You bet I have!'

'Means I've a good reason to kill you.'

'Morgan!' a woman moaned. 'We have to . . .'

Edge thought there was a good chance the man was bluffing — that the ambushers who had taken over the farmstead would not have allowed the owner to keep his gun. But he could not be sure the nervous and elderly sounding man was still unarmed now that the ambushers were dead. There was a much better than fifty-fifty chance such a man who farmed this isolated piece of terrain was no crack shot.

So he began his move just as the woman started to shout

the name: and had taken two long strides toward the corner of the frame house when Silas Martin fired the first shot with the Winchester.

The window shattered.

The woman screamed.

The man snarled: 'Sonofabitch!'

Martin fired again, the bullet cracking through the open doorway to clang against metal.

'Please! Stop it! Stop it! We don't have any gun!'

It was the man who pleaded, his words competing with further explosions as Martin continued to give Edge covering fire.

Then the half-breed reached the cover of the corner of the house, the Remington in his hand but unfired.

One more shot cracked out from beneath the depot boardwalk, hissed through the broken window, ricocheted off metal and produced a wet sounding, sharply curtailed groan from the man in the house.

Martin shouted something, but his voice was too weak to carry to Edge.

'You bastards! You bastards! You killed him! You killed my man!'

The woman was a fat blonde of forty plus whose voice was suddenly louder and shriller as she burst from the doorway of the house. She was naked from the waist up, her lower body covered by a piece of material tied with string around her hips. It gaped wide to expose her flabby thighs as she ran – her arms stretched out to their fullest extent in front of her.

'Don't try it, lady!' Edge snarled, stepping out from around the corner as the woman threw herself down close to the nearest dead man.

But even when he loosed a shot, which kicked snow up at the side of her face, she ignored him. Her hands fisted around the dead man's discarded Winchester and she used his body as a rest to draw a bead on Silas Martin.

Perhaps she would not have hit the wounded old man, who had hauled himself painfully up from under the boardwalk and was now leaning against it, using the half-breed's empty Winchester as a makeshift crutch for additional support.

But Edge could not take the chance. His first shot had been fired from the hip. Now he took careful aim along his outstretched arm, and squeezed the trigger just as the woman completed the pump action of the rifle.

The bullet blasted killing entry into her skull through the left temple. It did not have the power to exit from behind her forehead. The reaction of her nervous system caused her to complete a half roll — off her belly, up on to her side and then sprawling, arms spreadeagled, on to her back. Her large, saggy breasts with the nipples distended by contact with the cold snow lost bulk and looked young and firm. Her lower body and legs remained decently covered by the blanket wrapped around her. The death mask fixed her features into an expression of hysterical grief.

'Stella! It ain't true! I ain't killed!'

The man who staggered from the doorway, blood seeping from a neck wound to soak into his shirt collar, was about fifty. Tall and very thin, with glazed eyes and spittle running through the bristles on his jaw. He stumbled to a point midway between the door and the dead woman and then halted. He shook his head violently, which seemed to clear his mind and his vision. Then dropped hard to his knees and began to beat at the snowy ground with his fists. Droplets of blood flew away from his neck wound to spot the whiteness.

'Why?' he wailed.

'She was aiming to shoot my boss,' Edge said softly, advancing on the kneeling man as Silas Martin began to stagger away from the boardwalk.

The distraught man appeared not to hear the words. 'Why us? We never did no harm to nobody! Why we gotta be made to suffer this way?' He heard the half-breed's footfalls or sensed his presence, and ceased his frenetic beating at the ground. Resting on his knees and forearms, he screwed his bleeding neck around to gaze helplessly up at the tall, lean figure towering over him. For a few moments he struggled with a memory:

then his eyes filled with hatred as he recalled Edge as the man he had tried to bluff into surrender. 'One way I'll die happy, mister,' he snarled.

'How's that, feller?'

'Iffen I live just long enough to see you swingin' from the end of a rope, you murderin' sonofabitch!'

'Long life to you, feller,' the half-breed said, and pursed his lips as he shifted his gaze toward the hobbling figure of Silas Martin. 'On account that a man in my line of work might just end up being that kinda highered hand.'

CHAPTER SEVEN

'IT DON'T make no difference to the hate I got for you, mister,' Morgan Lockwood growled. 'But I guess you done my Stella a favour, puttin' that bullet in her head.'

Edge and Silas Martin were warm for the first time since leaving Denver: the heat emanating from the fire in the cooking range of the farmhouse kitchen. But the old man was unaware of this small comfort, for he was unconscious: sprawled out on his back on the bare boarding of the kitchen floor, his head rested on a pillow. His plumpish torso was naked, except for strips of linen sheets which were bound around his chest. His face was red again, the unhealthiness of this high colour emphasised by the doughty whiteness of the skin of his upper body. His breathing was regular but shallow. There was a .25 calibre bullet from his own revolver imbedded so deeply in his right side that it was probable a surgeon with the best available equipment would not be able to save his life.

Edge had not tried to probe for the bullet: had simply cleaned the wound with hot water, poured a slug of Lockwood's whiskey into the hole, and dressed it. It was as the liquor seared and soaked into the bloody tissue that the old man screamed and passed out.

Even this treatment had been delayed, at Martin's own insistence — that while he kept Lockwood covered with Edge's Remington, the half-breed should go retrieve the crated casket. Aware that such a delay would make no ultimate difference, Edge had done this, using the homesteader's flatbed wagon and two horses: having to pile up snow behind the wagon then roping both horses to the crate to drag it aboard. The corpse of Mrs Martin was now in the barn, still on the wagon.

'They gave her a bad time?' the half-breed responded to the

emaciated man's opening, which was the first thing Lockwood had said since he had got up off his knees and come into the house.

He had led his pair of unwelcome guests into the small kitchen, lit a lamp and started a fire in the range. For the whole time, while Edge eased the clothing off Martin's upper body and took a look at the bullet wound, Lockwood had acted as if he were alone — had used the first pan of boiled water to bathe the congealing blood off the furrow which a ricocheting shell had dug across the side of his neck.

He sat now where he had always sat, on a hard seated, straight backed chair at the table in the centre of the room. Edge had claimed the cushioned rocker to one side of the range.

Outside, the four dead lay where they had fallen on the snow, stiffening quickly in the bitterly cold air of the early morning hours.

'Had her two times each,' Lockwood answered, staring down at the splayed fingers of his work-roughened hands which he pressed against the table top. 'One of 'em held a gun on me all the time. But least they didn't make me watch. Kept me in the parlour. Had Stella tied to the bed in the other room. Cried a lot at first, she did. But then it was like she was struck dumb. I reckon somethin' went in her mind. Could be she'd never have got over what they done to her. So maybe you did her a favour.'

'What happened, feller?' Edge asked, rising to take the boiling coffee pot off the range. He unhooked two china mugs from pegs on the dresser.

'To her?'

'No. Over at the depot and here at the house. When they first came to Butcherville.'

He set the mugs on the table and filled both to the brim. He carried his own mug of the strong, steaming brew back to the rocker and sat down, after placing the pot on the side of the range to keep warm.

'Any reason I should answer your questions, mister?' Until now the skinny farmer with the weak looking grey eyes and

70

thinning grey hair had been speaking with a dull tone, as if out of a private world of misery. But as he said this he shifted his gaze toward Edge and the words he spoke were harsh with deep felt bitterness.

The half-breed pursed his lips. 'You seem like a man who needs to talk. Nothing else you have to say will interest me. Not a lot of point to talking if no one listens.'

The fight went out of him and he dropped his head to stare at his hands again. 'Stella was good at listenin'. You don't find that in many women.'

He glanced across at the half-breed again and found his gaze trapped by a level stare of glinting blue indifference. When he escaped, he accused tonelessly: 'I think I liked 'em three bastards out there better than you, mister. Least they talked halfway civil to me when they wasn't rapin' Stella.'

'They fix you a cup of coffee, feller?'

Lockwood leaned forward, lowered his face over the mug and spat a stream of saliva into the coffee.

'Your loss.'

'Worth it, mister! A man that has feelin's gotta relieve 'em the best way he can. If I spit in your eye, I reckon you'd kill me. Right?'

'You got anything left to live for, feller?'

'Not now Stella's dead I ain't.'

Edge nodded. 'Then I wouldn't kill you.'

Lockwood grimaced but did not look directly into the half-breed's face this time. 'How's a man get to be so hard and mean as you, mister?'

Edge extended a forefinger to point down at Silas Martin. 'An hour or so, he's going to wake up or die. Whichever, I'll be leaving then.'

'What's that got to do with it?'

'Means I don't have the time to answer your question.'

Silence descended on the small, warm kitchen, marred only by the breathing of the unconscious old man. Until Morgan Lockwood spoke again.

'They came last evenin'. Just as dusk was fallin'. Rode in

71

on the north trail. Didn't stop by this place, for which me and Stella was mighty grateful. They didn't look like the kinda company folks want to entertain. Even though we hadn't seen anyone 'ceptin' Dave Hardin' since the big snow came.'

There was a dullness back in his tone: of a man needing desperately to talk but resenting the impassive audience which was all he could command.

'Couple of passenger trains had come through from Denver by then, but nobody'd gotten off while the tanks were bein' filled. Just too damn cold for folks, I guess. But a couple of real weird lookin' guys got outta the caboose of the iron carrier that pulled into the depot.'

Edge continued to sip the hot, strong coffee without giving any indication that his interest had abruptly deepened in the story Lockwood was telling. Not that the homesteader looked up from his splayed hands to see if his words were producing any reaction from the half-breed.

'Fancy dressed foreigners. Chinese, I'd guess. Like a lot of the guys they used to build the railroad. But these two looked a lot richer than 'em workers. Anyway, that's when the trouble started over to the depot. Couldn't see nor hear much from this place, but got told about it by one of 'em guys while the other two was using Stella.'

Silas Martin groaned and rolled his head from side to side. Edge and Lockwood both looked at the old man, but he quietened again. His breathing began to sound stronger.

'All on account of his box, ain't it, mister?'

'They did your wife wrong, but they told you right, feller.'

Lockwood sighed, lifted his mug in both hands and almost had his lips to the rim when he saw the globule of saliva floating on the surface of the coffee.

'Just not your night,' Edge said.

'There's more in the pot.'

'Later.'

'Hard and mean as they come.'

The half-breed rocked forward and topped up his own mug.

'I told you, there's no time to talk about me. The trouble at the depot.'

Lockwood licked his dry lips and began to study his hands again. 'Seems these three that rode in from the north figured to ride on the train. But the fancy dressed foreigners got 'em to change their minds. Come down off the caboose with guns on the brakeman, which kept the engineer and fireman and Dave Hardin' in line. The three guys you shot, they didn't do nothin' to stop it. Guys with an eye for the main chance, they was. Like you.'

'But not so hard and mean.'

'You can say that again.'

'Try not to repeat myself. It wastes time. Sooner you get through, sooner you get fresh coffee.'

'Don't do me no favours.'

'Used up all my goodwill on your woman, feller.'

Lockwood drew in a deep breath and seemed set to snarl an angry retort. But then sighed back into depression. 'All right. The foreigners let the train take on water and leave. Stayed on board 'emselves after they made a deal with 'em three you shot. Give 'em money — a hundred bucks — and promised four hundred more iffen they'd get the box off you and the old timer. And bring it to the next water stop east. That's at Olsen Creek. Train hadn't been pulled outta the depot more than five minutes when Stella and me got Dave killed.'

Silas Martin groaned again, but only Edge glanced at him this time. The man at the table was too deeply enmeshed in bitter memories to be distracted by the present.

'Far as we knowed, not havin' seen nor heard nothin', there was only Dave over to the depot. Usually, he came over here to supper every night. But what with trains comin' outta Denver thick and fast, we figured he was too busy. So we took him a plate over. Just got to open the door when Dave shouted somethin'. Never will know what it was. Warnin' to keep out, I guess. Anyway, one of them three you shot was a real nervous guy. Me and Stella could see right across the office into the

73

room at the back. Saw this guy swing his arm at Dave. Looked like a punch. But next thing Dave was rollin' around on the floor spreadn' his blood all over.

'Ain't much more to tell, mister. The three of 'em brought 'emselves and their horses over here. Ate the supper Stella'd cooked and then started in on rapin', sleepin' and talkin'. Until your train came in. Have that fresh coffee now?'

Edge nodded toward the pot.

'How far away is Olsen Creek?'

'Seventy-five miles,' Lockwood answered as he rose from the table and went to the sink to empty the cold coffee before approaching the range. 'Unmanned halt. Just a place by the track where the Union Pacific keep cordwood and water.'

He lifted the pot off the range and started to pour coffee into his mug.

The half-breed appeared to be deep in thought — was in fact briefly contemplating why Hitoshi and Zenko had decided to hire the trio of drifting gunmen. But he was conscious of the thin farmer standing four feet away from him: distrustful of the way Lockwood had become thirsty. So that, when the man made to hurl the scalding liquid, Edge was ready to combat the move.

The homesteader had time only to set down the near empty pot and swing back his right hand which was fisted around the mug. By then, the half-breed had forced his thighs hard against the seat of the chair — using the rocker action to power his rise and leap forward over the unconscious form of Silas Martin. Both his hands flew away from the arms of the chair.

Lockwood stumbled backward with a cry of alarm: which took on the shrillness of terror as Edge fixed a double handed grip on him. His right fisted around the man's wrist, forcing him to drop the mug. His left fastened on the scrawny throat, to choke off the scream.

Then he backed the man fast to the table and bent him over it. The homesteader trembled from head to toe, his weak eyes bulging and his mouth gaping wide. His free hand lay uselessly at his side and he made no attempt to struggle. When Edge released him, he remained sprawled across the table top. But it was despair rather than fear which dictated his complete lack of reaction.

'I wanted you to kill me, you sonofabitch,' he said hoarsely.

'I know. But we covered that.' The half-breed's total lack of expression had not been marred by even a flicker of emotion since Lockwood had telegraphed his intention to goad him into the attack.

'I ain't got the guts to kill myself, mister.' Tears welled up from his eyes and because he was lying flat out on his back the salty beads trickled from under the lids to the tops of his ears.

'That's a problem a lot of us have, feller.'

Lockwood raised his head off the table to look quizzically at the tall, lean man who backed away from him to sit down again in the rocker. 'You mean there's been times when you . . . ?'

'I'm a widower, too,' Edge supplied as his hooded, glinting eyes trapped the gaze of the man and provoked him into curious silence. He extended a forefinger toward Martin again. 'So is he. Figure his hurting will soon be over.'

Frowning, Lockwood rose slowly to his feet and then sat down on the chair at the table. For a long time the breathing of the unconscious Martin was the only sound in the room. As the homesteader pondered a way to capitalise on the glimpse of deep sadness which had been revealed to him during the moments the half-breed had allowed his guard of impassiveness to drop.

And as Edge recalled the unaccustomed hot anger which had gripped him when he saw the possibility that the old man might lose the corpse of his wife. Then how he had felt the need to leave his rifle with Silas Martin as a sign of good faith that he meant to return the casket to the wounded old man.

Perhaps at the beginning the five-dollar-a-day fee had had some bearing on why he had accepted the job with Martin. Or maybe that had merely been a cynical excuse he had made — to himself as well as others. For was it not true that the relationship between a man and his wife was the only association for which he had any respect? No, even beyond that. The grief a man felt for his dead wife.

Certainly the loss of Beth had affected him worse than the death of Jamie. Jamie was his brother, deserving of love and respect because of blood ties. The feelings between a man and a woman in love had to be stronger and deeper, based as they were on the abstract foundations of trust.

After Jamie's brutal death, thoughts of suicide had never entered his head. But when he discovered Beth's rancid, stinking corpse . . .

He buried her decently and it had required little effort to do this. Silas Martin wanted the same thing for the remains of his wife, but was not finding it easy to achieve such a simple aim. Which had aroused a feeling of affinity within Edge — strong enough for the half-breed to discount his initial suspicion that the old man had a less honourable motive for getting the casket to New York state.

So it was memories of an old and personal grief which Morgan Lockwood had seen fleetingly displayed upon the sooted and bristled features of Edge — recollections of the death of Beth and his responses to it, resurrected by the disparate actions of Martin and the homesteader in similar circumstances. One man deserving of what little sympathy the half-breed was capable of feeling and the other — who was content to leave the near naked body of his wife to freeze in the open night — not worth the price of a bullet or effort to break his neck.

As Lockwood's mind took hold of an idea somewhere close to the truth, he looked across at Edge with a sneer on his lips. 'She was no loss, I bet.'

'Who?'

'Your wife. Kinda woman that'd marry a man like you, she'd be no good. Outta a dancehall. Or maybe a cathouse. Yeah, I bet she was a whore!'

'Keep talking, feller,' Edge said evenly, thin lips and narrow eyes offering no more of a clue to his thoughts than his voice did.

76

'Couldn't been no decent woman. Outta the same kind of gutter you come from. She ever tell you how many men screwed her before you? What she die of, mister? The clap, I wouldn't mind bettin'.'

He laughed his excitement through the sneer as he watched Edge rise slowly from the rocker, step across the unconscious Martin and move to the table.

'A whore she was! Ain't that the truth? A fifty cent piece of ass outta a cathouse! Stinkin' of every drunken bum that ever shot his load into her.'

Lockwood's voice rose to a shriller pitch and spittle sprayed from his quivering lips as the half-breed halted on the other side of the table from him. And drew the Remington from its holster.

'I got it right, ain't I? Or else you'd be burnin' up with temper!'

Edge's thumb clicked back the hammer.

The skinny man across from him tried to hurl more insults, but the laughter of triumph filled his scrawny throat and exploded out into the small, warm kitchen. He threw his arms wide to the sides and screwed his eyes tight shut.

The handgun roared, the report amplified in the confines of the room.

Lockwood curtailed his laughter.

'I won, you sonofabitch!' he yelled. 'I forced you to kill me! I beat you and ...'

He screamed then, as the pain burst through the numbing effect of the bullet's impact and seared to every nerve ending in his system. He snapped open his eyes and tore his gaze away from the smoking muzzle of the Remington to look down at the blossoming red stain at the crotch of his pants.

Edge waited for the scream to give way to sobs. Which happened as Lockwood dropped back on to his chair with a force that almost tipped it over.

'Nobody had Beth before me, feller,' he said then. 'And you'll never have another woman. Don't ever believe again that rhyme about names not hurting anybody.'

Lockwood was whimpering now, probably not hearing the half-breed's words as he stared down at his cupped hands, which filled with blood as he nursed his injury.

'Edge,' Silas Martin groaned, weakly and painfully. 'Was that a shot I just heard?'

'Yeah.'

'You all right?'

'Fine.' Edge holstered the Remington and went down on his haunches besides the old man.

'Then what?'

'Lockwood was shooting off his mouth, Silas,' the half-breed replied. 'I aimed lower.'

CHAPTER EIGHT

THEY rolled away from the Butcherville farmstead at first light with Edge up on the wagon seat and Silas Martin wrapped in several blankets on the back — wedged as comfortably as possible between the crate and the side of the flatbed.

The half-breed had shaved and eaten a breakfast of bacon and beans. The old man had got down a half cup of coffee before he coughed it up again, along with pieces of the last meal he had in Denver. He was living on borrowed time but possessed the kind of willpower that would ensure he got the most days, hours, minutes and seconds out of the loan before he finally succumbed to the inevitable.

Behind the wagon moving slowly alongside the railroad toward the leading arc of the rising sun, Morgan Lockwood lay on the double bed he had shared with his wife and willed himself to die. But deep down knew that help would come before he starved to death in the small, cold farmhouse. Out on the field in front of the house, the three dead gunmen and the half naked woman still lay crumpled on the snow. While across the track, in the back room of the depot building, Dave Harding's corpse began to stink of decay.

'That was a real terrible thing you did to that man back there,' Martin said mournfully after the sun had hauled itself completely clear of the horizon and the buildings of Butcherville were merely small dark dots in the far distance.

Edge, driving the wagon with the brim of his hat pulled low over his forehead against the glare of the sun, made no reply.

'It was an accident, what happened to me,' the wounded old man went on after he had replenished the strength expended on his first effort to speak. 'That engineer was scared I'd do something stupid and get his partner killed. He was

79

just trying to get the gun off me. He didn't mean to shoot me.'

Again the half-breed held his peace.

'And we shouldn't have stolen his wagon and team. I could have paid him.'

Edge looked briefly back over his shoulder, to where only the old man's pale and already thinning face showed above the blankets. 'You still have to talk, don't you?'

The wagon jolted and Martin bit hard on his lower lip as the movement triggered a fresh wave of pain from the area where the bullet was lodged in his flesh. 'Not just for the hell of it. I hired you, son. So I feel responsible for what happened back there. The Lockwoods were innocent bystanders. You killed her and gelded him. There was no need for that.'

Edge was facing front again, detecting a faint warmth in the rays of the sun which struck his lower face. The ruts cut in the snow by the wagon wheels began to crumble into twin lines of dirty coloured slush.

'I figured I was doing you a favour when I shot her, feller.'

'She'd never have hit me over that distance!' Martin interrupted grimly.

'But that doesn't matter anyway,' the half-breed went on in the same even tone. 'Her husband reckons she's better off dead, after what those drifters did to her.'

The old man vented a weak snort of disgust. 'An excuse after the event. I hope it helps you to sleep better at nights.'

'Maybe it will,' Edge allowed.

'Even though you shot the balls off the man who gave it to you.'

'I didn't ask him for anything, feller.'

Exhaustion, pain or the realisation that he was beating his head against a brick wall caused Silas Martin to sink into suffering silence. More than five minutes passed before Edge spoke.

'Not much in this world I give a damn about. My own life. The job I'm being paid to do. The memory of my wife. That's why what happened happened back there. And we didn't steal the wagon and team. Lockwood's got three new horses, all of them better than these two. And the hundred bucks the Japanese put up for the ambush will more than pay for a new wagon.'

There was no response to this and when he glanced over his shoulder again he saw that the old man was sleeping. A dying man wedged against the side of the crate containing the casket in which lay the dead body of his wife. The living man up on the seat faced forward again and began to rake the surrounding plains country with slitted eyes gazing out from the shadow of his hat brim. The terrain was too flat the morning visibility too good for danger to be lurking within effective range of the slow wagon. But Edge had to occupy his mind with something: to keep out of his thoughts an insistent demand to consider who aboard the flatbed was the most fortunate. The living, the dying or the dead?

Mai Lin's troubles were over.

Silas Martin had one final task to complete and then would be able to rest easy.

Edge?

'No contest, feller,' he muttered to himself between exposed teeth clenched in a sardonic grin. 'It may be a dog's life but you're one sonofabitch who ain't ready to leave it yet.'

'What's that you say?' the old man asked as he was jolted awake in time to hear the half-breed's voice without being able to discern what he said.

'Nothing, Silas. Thinking aloud is all. And barking up the wrong tree.'

During the three days and nights it took them to reach the Union Pacific fuel stop at Olsen Creek, Martin was asleep more than he was awake. And his ability to rest, even aboard the jolting and pitching wagon, helped him to cling on to the final thin threads of his life. But he was unable to eat and each evening and morning when Edge took a look at his wound the festering flesh was uglier and smelled worse. He got weaker and paler with each hour that passed. And sometimes during the warm, sunlit days it seemed to the half-breed that he could actually see the old man becoming thinner.

Edge followed the railroad all the way to Olsen Creek and did not see a train until the early morning of the third day out of Butcherville, when a smudge of dark woodsmoke against the rising sun caught his eye.

There was a stand of scrub pine four hundred feet north of the track and he used the crack of the whip to urge the horses into a gallop toward the timber. The noise and speed roused Martin to a frantic world of pain and dust and he yelled questions at Edge, who remained silent until the wagon and team came to a halt in the cover of the trees. By that time the old man was unable to make any sounds except groans in response to the fires of agony searing his body.

'Train coming, feller,' the half-breed explained as he jumped down from the seat and moved into the trees.

'What scares you about that?' Martin managed to growl.

'The U.P. might have heard what I did to their bridge,' Edge answered, watching the dot under the smoke smudge take the form of a locomotive, enlarging in perspective as the engineer urged maximum speed from his charge.

'And their brakeman!'

The tall, lean man crouching among the trees bit back on an angry retort: indulging Silas Martin as a dying man who was entitled to feel deeply for those who had recently gone the way he was due to take.

Then the thud of pistons, the rattle of spinning wheels and the clanking of heavily laden cars filled the warming air of the plains morning.

There were, in fact, two large four-six-o locomotives: hauling a double length string of box and flatcars. Men gazed disconsolately out of the open doors of two boxcars. The flatcars were loaded with timber and rails.

The entire train roared past the stand of pines in less than a minute. The ground ceased to shake, the clamour faded, then the caboose went from sight into the distant west. The smell of woodsmoke remained in the air for almost as long as the wispy blackness against the blue sky.

Martin was morosely silent for several minutes after Edge had set the wagon rolling. Then offered:

'I'm sorry, son.'

'For what?'

'Criticising you for what you are — the way you get things done.'

'I got a thick skin, feller. Except for the part that covers an old grief.'

'If you weren't the way you are, I guess we wouldn't have made it this far. While there's people like me, there'll always be people like you. I should be grateful to you, instead of keep putting you down.'

'I'll accept gratitude from somebody who doesn't have the money, feller,' the half-breed told him. 'So far you owe me twenty dollars.'

'If I die before you get paid, there's money in my hip pocket,' Martin said, resentful of Edge's response to his apology.

'Obliged.'

'But I don't plan on cashing in my chips until we get to where we're going.'

'I believe you.'

The water tower at Olsen Creek showed first, the big tank crouched above the curvature of the seemingly limitless prairie of the Colorado-Kansas border country. Then the topmost layer of cordwood stacked on the other side of the track from the tower. The only other feature of the halt was a small shack at the side of the tower supports.

The creek for which the place was named was just a dried up bed but there was obviously a water course beneath it: for a metal pipe came up from the cracked ground, entered the shack and then rose to the tank at the top of the tower. The shack apparently housed a steam pump. The telegraph wire ran across the roof of the shack and between the tower support timbers without interruption.

'How does it look, son?' Silas Martin asked, his hands out from under the blankets and trembling as they gripped the half-breed's Winchester.

83

'We're two hundred feet away and it looks as quiet as it sounds,' Edge told him, driving with the reins in one hand, his right palm draped over the butt of the holstered Remington.

Both men were sweating, more heavily than was merited by the heat of the sun. Dust from beneath the rolling wheels of the wagon rose and clung to the beads of perspiration suspended in their bristles.

Silas Martin was hurting inside.

Edge's belly was ice cold with the fear of sudden death. But there had been no other way to handle the approach to Olsen Creek. The small shack, the twenty-feet high pile of logs and the water tower which rose skywards at least another ten feet provided the only cover of any consequence for as far as the eye could see. Short of making an immensely wide detour to north or south, there had been no alternative to a direct and open advance on the fuel halt.

A hundred feet from the log pile, the two horses in the traces pricked their ears and raised their heads, nostrils quivering. Another horse whinnied.

'Trouble,' Edge rasped.

'Hell,' Martin groaned.

'Don't wanna kill no one!' a man shouted.

The half-breed had hauled on the reins to halt the team and drawn the Remington halfway out of the holster. His glinting eyes were focused on the woodpile, for it was behind this that the horse had sounded the warning.

The short, fat man who stepped into view on the track side of the logs had a Winchester levelled from his shoulder. But he was not the one who made the claim. This man was halfway up the tower, leaning into sight from behind one of the stout timber struts. He had a matching repeater rifle. He was also short, but far less heavy than the man on the ground. Both were in their mid-forties, with faces burnished by weather and dressed western style in dark hued clothing that showed many signs of hard wear. Each wore a bushy black moustache that drooped to either side of the mouth.

'Feller on the seat ease the gun outta the holster slow and

toss it to the side. One in the back heave the rifle over the side.'

While the spokesman, who had a deep south acent, held his position, his partner advanced along the side of the log pile.

'What's the situation, Edge?' Martin rasped.

'Bad. Do what he tells you.'

The old man was reluctant to surrender the Winchester. But did so after he heard the Remington clunk against the ground. The revolver had gone to the left. The rifle went right.

'Fine, Rubin,' the man from behind the logs drawled. 'You can come on down now. I got him covered.'

'Be careful of the one in the back, Ralph. He might have a handgun under them blankets.'

'He won't do nothin', Rubin. Not if he wants his partner to keep on livin'. Get down outta the back, mister.'

'I can't.'

Rubin began to climb down from the tower, with frequent anxious glances to where Ralph stood aiming the rifle at Edge over a range of twenty feet.

Ralph scowled. 'Don't you tell me can't, mister. You do like I say.'

'Goddamnit, I have a bullet inside me!' Silas Martin snapped.

'That right?' Ralph asked Edge.

'Take a look,' the half-breed invited. 'Though I guess you'll smell what it's doing to him before you get close enough to see.'

Ralph was suspicious. 'Reckon I'll wait for Rubin to get over here first.'

'What do you want, feller?'

Ralph had a weak grin which made him look younger. 'What do you think? Money. Valuables. Me and Rubin, we're the have nots. Hopin' you and your partner are a couple of haves.'

'Just that?' Martin asked, surprised. 'You're not working for anybody?'

'For us,' Ralph supplied as Rubin drew level with him. 'Keep the big one covered.'

He moved wide round the team and wagon to reach the rear.

'Silas has a small calibre gun under the blankets,' Edge supplied.

'Damn you, Edge!' the old man snarled as Ralph, who had been about to delve under the blankets covering him, abruptly stabbed the muzzle of the rifle into his chin.

'If it's my money or my life, I'd rather be poor,' the half-breed rasped, his hooded eyes focused upon the knuckle of Rubin's right forefinger curled to the rifle trigger.

'It ain't true what's said,' Rubin drawled while Ralph held his Winchester one handed and reached under the blankets to take the My Friend revolver from Martin's reluctant grasp.

'What?' Edge asked.

'That a fool and his money are soon parted. You're a wise man. Dig deep and toss out your dollars.'

The balance of what the half-breed had been paid for the Big-T cattle drive was in the hip pocket of his pants. He delved his hand in and drew it out slowly, fisted around the roll of bills. His slitted eyes never shifted from the curled finger and the ugly black hole of the rifle muzzle above.

Behind him, Ralph said: 'Rest easy, old timer. I'll get yours. Man in your condition shouldn't do nothin' 'ceptin' lay still.'

'What's wrong with him?' Rubin asked, his attention not wandering from Edge for a moment as the hefty roll of dollars sailed through the air to hit the ground at his feet with a rich-sounding thud.

'Been shot. He smells real bad.'

'Tough.'

'What's in the box?'

'Something that smells worse than Silas,' Edge supplied. 'Corpse of his wife. She's been dead a few weeks.'

'What the hell are you doing . . .'

'Forget it, Ralph,' Rubin cut in. 'You through back there?'

'Yeah. Five hundred maybe. And a gold watch. The big guy got any watch, rings, stuff like that?'

'He ain't the type,' Rubin answered, abruptly more nervous than he had been as he climbed down from the water tower.

The utter coldness in the half-breed's glinting blue eyes and the total lack of expression in the lines of his other features were starting to get to Rubin.

'We better take their guns, uh?'

'Of course we take their friggin' guns. Then pick up this money over here. Hurry it up.'

'You figure to hold up a train?' Edge asked as Ralph scuttled around the wagon, collecting the two revolvers and the Winchester.

'Nah. Just came by here to get fresh water. Saw you headin' this way. Glad we waited.' Talking seemed to ease his jangling nerves.

'You see anybody else around here, feller?'

'Why would anybody hang around this asshole of nowhere?'

'Expected to met up with a couple of Orientals is all.'

'You're too late or too early. Ain't been nobody here for three hours.'

'Obliged.'

'Jesus, Rubin!' Ralph gasped as he stopped to pick up the half-breed's bankroll. 'Did we get lucky! We ain't never had this much before.'

'Two thousand, feller,' Edge said. 'Hard come by. Easy gone.'

'Too damn easy for my likin',' Ralph growled, suddenly as anxiously suspicious of the half-breed's manner as was his partner.

'Figure I'm worth more than that is all.'

'Keep figurin' that, mister,' Rubin muttered, and began to back away along the side of the track.

He halted at the corner of the pile of logs and said something to Ralph, who nodded and quickened his pace. Stretched seconds dragged through time while Ralph was out of sight. Then hooves hit the ground and the fat man appeared astride a horse, with Rubin's mount on a lead line.

Rubin continued to level his rifle from the shoulder at Edge, ignoring Silas Martin who had struggled to sit up and turn around to see what was happening. So the fat man had no

87

trouble in drawing his Colt — and blasting a bullet into the nape of his thin partner's neck.

'God in heaven!' Martin gasped.

'And there's a lot wrong with the world,' Edge muttered.

'We never stole this much before!' Ralph exclaimed. 'Too much to share.'

He never took his gaze away from Edge as he slid from his saddle and stooped over the corpse of his partner. He holstered his own Colt and used Rubin's revolver to keep his confidence high while he pushed the dead man's rifle into the boot on the now spare horse. Then he remounted and wheeled both horses — to lunge them into an immediate gallop.

Dust from beneath the pumping hooves drifted lazily to settle on the covering of sheened crimson that was spread over the back of Rubin's head: and dulled it, changing its colour to black.

'I've never seen anything so cold blooded as that in my whole life,' Silas Martin gasped, having to grip the top of the wagon side to keep sitting up: staring after the dust cloud that marked the eastward progress of Ralph.

'If you've got enough life left, I aim to top it, Silas,' Edge rasped, taking up the reins to drive the team to the water tower.

'No, son! Forget him. I haven't got the time to . . .'

The half-breed dropped to the ground and a cold stare from the slits of his eyes was enough to drive the pale, thin faced old man into silence.

Then, as Edge turned his broad back and moved across the track to the water hose, Martin said: 'If that's the way you feel, I'm in no position to argue.'

'It's what I don't feel bothers me, feller.'

'What you don't?' came the puzzled response.

Edge placed the palm of a hand on his empty his pocket. 'I don't feel any two grand.'

CHAPTER NINE

EVEN after the team had been watered and Edge had seen that Silas Martin was tightly wrapped in the blankets and wedged securely on the back of the wagon again, Ralph was still in sight — he and the two horses a composite dark dot far to the south east.

Then, shortly after the wagon had started to roll, the old man crying aloud his pain as the wheels jolted over the track, the quarry went from sight: swallowed up by mere distance across the vast mid-western plain.

'Let him go, son,' Martin said as the impassive-faced half-breed took a fix on a low rise that gave him an approximate bearing on the point at which Ralph had disappeared. 'Let him go and I'll make good your loss.'

His voice was weak, the words having to be forced out of a private world of agony. But the man who heard them was able to detect the misery of defeat in the strained whisper.

'You're as broke as I am, Silas,' he replied.

'When we get to where we're going there'll be money. Lots of it.'

Edge looked back and down at the fatally wounded man. The strong, warm sunlight fell on a face with screwed shut eyes and teeth bared in a tight grimace of agony.

'Syracuse, New York state, feller?'

'Right. Like I said.' The words, forced through the clenched teeth, were almost inaudible through the hiss of expelled breath that drove them out. 'And I'm going to make it.'

'Not aboard this wagon, feller. It's too rough and too slow.'

'You're making it slower. Going the wrong way.'

'Anything you can do about it, feller?'

'Regret I ever hired you!' He managed to inject a harsh tone of anger into the response.

'So you do that, Silas.'

'You're hard and mean, Edge! Just like that farmer told you!'

'Hard up for sure,' the half-breed answered. 'So I can't afford to be generous.'

Martin was silent for a long time, while Edge concentrated upon keeping the wagon on a course that would take it about two miles right of the rise. The half-breed did not forget about his suffering employer, to the extent that he held the team to an easy walk and steered to avoid the worst of the humps and hollows that would have juddered the flatbed and ignited new fires of agony in the old man's punished body. But his main concern was now a personal one.

A twist of cruel fate might rob him and he had come to accept such a loss with equanimity. For there was no way he could gain revenge against an abstract concept. But a living, breathing man like the fat little Ralph: that was a different proposition. Unless the hold-up man paid the price for robbing Edge, the half-breed would feel he had lost far more than mere money and guns. He would be stripped of his pride. Another abstract concept, but one he would risk his life to protect. For if he lost this, he would be forced to regard himself as no better than the man he was tracking.

When he reached the point on the prairie upon which he had taken the fix, he had to look for signs left by the two horses. A chore he welcomed, for once again it was necessary to make an effort to close his mind against unwelcome thoughts — that his selfish pursuit of a personal principle which sidetracked him from the job he had been hired to do, by a man who was close to death, maybe placed him as low down on the human scale as Ralph.

'Edge,' Martin croaked as the half-breed peered far ahead to where a line of low hills showed faintly in the shimmering heat haze.

'Yeah, Silas?'

'He could have killed us. The way he did his partner.'

'People make mistakes all the time, feller.'

90

'You included, son.'

'Was just thinking I'm a long way from being perfect.'

'Everybody is. Think some more. Even if you find him in this wide open country, he's armed and you aren't. He won't leave you alive to follow him a second time. And you told him and his partner you reckoned your life was worth more than two thousand dollars.'

'I told the truth, Silas. Figure that right now my life is worth living.'

'What's that supposed to mean?'

'That if I don't kill the bastard I won't be able to live with myself.'

'Vanity!' Martin rasped, then moderated his tone, perhaps because he could not sustain high emotion. 'Take care, son. You know what comes before a fall?'

'Yeah,' Edge growled, and spat off the side of the wagon. 'A summer.'

'I'm in no mood for jokes,' the old man retorted, and groaned as a wheel bounced over a rock.

'And I'm in no mood to take a fall, feller,' the half-breed growled. 'I'm down as far as I can go.'

'No you're not, son. A grave goes deeper. And it could be you're digging your own.'

'You got anything to say I don't already know?'

The old man did not reply for long moments. Then he sighed. 'I guess not, by your reckoning. A man like you thinks he knows it all.'

'So save your breath, Silas. You haven't got enough left to waste it.'

Martin groaned again, but with misery rather than pain. Edge sensed the brown eyes staring up at his back, emanating hatred and frustration: and he allowed himself a brief, tight grin. The old man would keep quiet now, silently nursing his resentment and willing himself to stay alive. Which might give him a few more minutes, hours or even days. Which was maybe more than the contents of any doctor's bag could have given him.

As the sun rose higher and got hotter, the heat haze thickened. But the wagon had rolled far enough into the south east for the line of low hills to stay in sight. The sign left by Ralph's mount and the horse on a lead line marked a course toward a fold between the two highest rises.

At about midday, Silas Martin vented an odd sounding growl. But it was only a vocal reaction to some image that flickered through his mind as he lay wedged on the back of the wagon, resting on the line between sleep and unconsciousness. When the growl was curtailed, the old man resumed his shallow breathing. The recent thinning of his face was clear to see, but the paleness of his complexion was hidden: by the trail dust that adhered to the sweat which constantly pumped from his pores — the saline beads like drops of his diminishing strength being squeezed out by the pain.

After snapping his head around in response to the strange sound, Edge avoided looking at Martin again. Only in this way was he able to suppress the guilt he felt.

Nearing the hills and then entering them under a sky growing dark with evening, the half-breed was conscious of two nagging concerns. Most urgent of these was that Ralph undoubtedly knew he was being trailed. For if Edge had been able to see him during the first few hours, then he had certainly been aware of the wagon rolling in his wake. On the open prairie there had been nothing he could do about his pursuers. And he had not tried, even by demanding more speed from his mount — the sign on the short grass and dusty bald patches revealed a constant, even pace. But here in the hollows and rises of the hilly area, with night falling fast, there was ample opportunity for the hold-up man to prepare and spring a trap.

Which was why Edge reined the weary team to a halt before the final crimson rays of the setting sun had faded from the western dome of the sky. The silence which closed in around him after hooves had ceased to clop and springs to creak was eerie in its seeming completeness. But it lasted for little more than two seconds: until Silas Martin sucked in some air and Edge allowed the breath to whistle out through his teeth. Then the wagon made small sounds as the horses moved a couple of feet forward to start cropping on grass.

The chosen spot was at the centre of a broad, shallow hollow surrounded by grassy slopes, the highest ground no more than forty feet above where the wagon was parked. A man atop any of the hills would have had a clear shot at the half-breed as he sat on the wagon seat, sucking tepid water from a canteen and raking his narrow-eyed gaze in every direction. But it was a chance Edge had to take and he took it. And when he survived, he gave brief consideration to the other point which concerned him, as he watered the horses and then released them from the traces.

There had been no sign to mark the border, but he felt sure that he had crossed from Colorado into Kansas some time during the afternoon. A fact which demanded his attention because of that long ago killing of Elliot Thombs. He had been in the state of Kansas only once before since he killed Thombs — at a time when he had been, perhaps, as close to death as was Silas Martin now. And only narrowly had escaped the posse which had sought to capture him.

But it was not fear of legal retribution which bothered him as he moved away from the stalled wagon and grazing horses. Instead, he considered the possibility of his ruling fate dealing out a more subtle form of justice — by having a fat little hold-up man fire a shot that would spill the life blood of Edge on the dusty soil of Kansas.

A mile beyond the parked wagon, he came to an abrupt halt, his moonlit features altering from their impassive set to take on the lines of a frown. He was halfway up a long, gentle incline, stepping directly into the hoofprints left by the two horses: his hooded eyes raking constantly from left to right to study the curved crest of the hill silhouetted in solid black against the star pricked sky.

He saw nothing to warn him of danger and his straining ears picked up no sound. And a half second later he realised it was his sense of smell which had brought him to an instinctive halt.

There was a fire somewhere close.

He remained erect as he started forward again: until he was in danger of being skylined. Then he went down on to all fours for a few yards, finally flat out on to his belly.

The smell of burning became stronger by the moment and he even heard the crackle of flames attacking wood before he reached the vantage point of the hill crest. And looked down at Ralph's night camp.

It was at the bottom of a narrow, north to south valley with grass on the slope falling away from where Edge watched, and low brush cloaking the other side. The fire had never been a large one and was now little more than a heap of softly glowing embers, which stirred, flamed and crackled only when they were fanned by a slight breeze which eddied along the valley.

The short, fleshy Ralph lay under his blankets on one side of the fire. The two horses were hobbled on the other side, close to the dark hump formed by the two saddles and spare bedroll. A coffee pot, a mug and a canteen were on the ground close to where Ralph slept — too early and too soundly for a man who knew he was being followed.

For stretched seconds, the half-breed directed his unblinking gaze at the heap of blankets — seconds that perhaps linked together to form a minute. Which was longer than a man could hold his breath. Long enough for Edge to be convinced that whatever caused the blankets to be shaped in human form was not breathing: and to decide that the Stetson at one end of the unfurled bedroll was not resting over the sleeping face of a man.

'I don't know it all, Silas,' the half-breed muttered as he shifted his attention to the brush covered slope beyond the camp site, 'but I ain't quite the fool that feller thinks I am.'

The brush was low growing but thick, merging as dark and solid with the ground on that side of the valley as the grass on the opposite slope. Edge guessed that Ralph would be concealed close to the camp, but this hunch was of no use to him.

For although he spent a full fifteen minutes peering at the area he was sure concealed the man, he saw no sign of life. Or if he did, any movement made by Ralph was covered by the gentle stirring of the foliage under the tug of the night breeze.

He withdrew from the hill crest then: moving far enough back from the slope so that he could rise to his full height. Then he headed north at a loping run, his faith in his plan increasing as the breeze freshened and dried the sweat of exertion on his lean face.

He did not alter direction until he was some six hundred yards beyond Ralph's night camp. He slowed down there, and was at his most cautious as he crested the rise and moved into the valley.

The embers of the cooking fire were almost out now, but the moon was as bright as ever. The horses, saddles and bedroll were clearly discernible as dark shapes against darkness. So he kept low and progressed in short spurts with long pauses in between. None of the small sounds he made would carry on the breeze to the camp. But a chance glance by a man with a repeater rifle in his hands would certainly mean the end. So now it was the sweat of fear which oozed from and dried on the half-breed's flesh.

Then he was across the valley and climbing up the opposite slope through the thorny, clothes-snagging, flesh-tearing brush. Still afraid, but with an easier mind — which allowed him to expose his teeth in a grin of evil relish as he considered the prospect of killing the man who robbed him.

A grin that became fixed and lacking in even sardonic humour when he reached the top of the rise and looked down into a hollow east of the valley. Saw a second night camp.

Two horses as at the one in the valley. Hobbled and unsaddled. But no fire and no patch of dark ashes to show where one had been. With unopened bedrolls stacked in the same heap with the saddles. There were no men in sight down in the hollow and there was no cover in which they could be concealed.

Moonlight illuminated the second camp as brightly as the

first — sufficient for the puzzled half-breed to see that there were no rifles in the saddle boots.

The absence of men and weapons established, Edge turned his attention back to Ralph's camp and started through the brush toward it. There were a thousand and one possibilities which might explain the horses and gear down in the hollow on the other side of the rise: the strongest of which was that Hitoshi and Zenko were the missing riders.

Beyond this, Edge did not project his thoughts into the unknown. For it was immaterial and therefore futile. The new development did not alter his intentions. Simply added to the danger of what he planned to do.

He advanced toward the valley camp on a diagonal line across the slope, his progress necessarily slow as the thorns clawed at his flesh and old, dead, dry twigs threatened to snap and reveal his position. So that it took him more than an hour to reach a point a hundred feet north of the camp and twenty feet up the slope from the valley bottom. In all that time, only the horses and wispy smoke from the dying fire made small movements on the open ground. While on the eastern slope the brush foliage continued to rustle, stirred out of inertia by the breeze from the north.

He reached his chosen position with blood from countless scratches mingling with the sweat beads on his face and hands. So that when he ran the back of a hand across his forehead, cheeks and jaw, the salty moisture soaked through the cut flesh to sting the tissue beneath. But the tension of controlled fear acted to swamp pain as he took from his jacket pockets the dry twigs he had collected at the top of the rise.

He made a pile of the twigs, delved for a match, struck it on his boot and held the flame in cupped hands beneath the kindling. He waited only long enough to ensure the twigs were burning before he turned and started back up the rise: able to move faster through the brush already flattened by his advance.

Behind him the small fire grew, the flames fanned into increasing ferocity by the chill night breeze. The brush began to crackle under the assault of the fire. Grey smoke was plucked

96

away from the flames and driven down the valley. Sparks rose, glowed brightly and died.

A man shouted. In a language the retreating half-breed did not understand. But the tone of alarm was clearly discernible. An answering burst of words was powered by anger.

Edge halted the fast crawl and looked back over his shoulder. He had struck the match less than thirty seconds before, yet the fire already had a firm hold on the brush: the flames broadening out across the valley side as eagerly as they advanced along it.

Shimmering columns of heat blurred parts of the scene ahead of the fire. Swirling smoke completely veiled other areas. But he glimpsed two brightly-garbed figures standing in the path of the hungry flames: swinging to left and right from the waist, rifles raking in the wake of frightened eyes searching for a target. Their mouths opened and closed, venting sounds which did not reach through the crackle of the fire to Edge's ears.

Then they moved their feet, heading in the direction the half-breed and hoped for: up the slope to escape the flames and gain the advantage of the high ground. Which left the way to Ralph's camp clear for Edge.

He got to his feet, whirled, and powered into a headlong run: down and across the slope, in the insubstantial cover of the leaping flames and swirling smoke. Twice his feet were snagged by curling, thorn-jagged brush branches and he was sent crashing full length to the ground. Each time, grimacing at the pain of impact and more blood spurting tears in his flesh, he took the opportunity to glance upward to his left. On the first occasion the flames and the smoke and the sweat and blood which dripped across his eyes blotted out the scene. But the next time he glimpsed the Japanese.

They had the more difficult route to cover, having to force their way upward through the brush. Conscious of the fire roaring at their backs. Aware, too, that the man who had set light to the brush might send killing shots toward them at any moment.

97

Down on the open ground of the valley floor, Edge length-ened his stride, gasping for breath and coughing violently as woodsmoke was sucked into his lungs with the air. Above him to the right, the slope was an expanse of charred vegetation, wisping with smoke here and there, behind the wall of fire that increased its speed with every foot it travelled. Ahead of him the two horses were over on their sides, sent crashing to the ground as the fire and smoke created panic in their brains and the hobbles on their forelegs prevented the rear and bolt they had sought to make. Their hindlegs flailed as their eyes bulged with terror, their necks strained upward, teeth bared.

The sudden appearance of the half-breed triggered a fresh wave of snorting from the helpless animals. He had to move in close to their dangerously kicking hooves to drag one of the saddles off the pile: only then was he able to slide the rifle from the boot.

He came to a skidding halt then, pumping the lever action of the Winchester and hearing the satisfying sound of a bullet being jacked into the breech.

Then another bullet thudded into horseflesh, silencing one of the animals which continued to thrash the ground and air in its death pangs.

Edge whirled and crouched, thudding the stock of the rifle to his shoulder and sighting with one narrowed, blue glinting eye along the barrel.

The report of the shot reached his ears: just as the muzzle and eye ceased to rake the hill top and he drew a bead on the target.

Both Hitoshi and Zenko had out-run the voracious flames: now stood on the top of the valley side, looking down at Edge across the blackened brush as the fire raged away to the south. Both had their rifles to their shoulders, one pumping the action after exploding the shot which missed the half-breed and killed the horse.

Edge aimed for the other Oriental and hurled himself for-ward as soon as he squeezed the trigger: seeing the puff of white muzzle smoke as the Japanese got off a shot.

The bullet from above came close enough to punch a hole in the half-breed's coat and shirt sleeves: searing the skin of his right arm without breaking it.

The Japanese made no defensive move and died for the mistake — taking the bullet in his chest, left of centre.

Edge hit the ground in the scant cover offered by the blanket draped form of the unmoving Ralph. As the Japanese fell, as stiffly as a tree, going from sight on the other side of the hill crest.

The empty shellcase ejected from the half-breed's Winchester was still spinning through the air as the surviving Oriental took aim — his target almost totally exposed from the higher vantage point.

But it was a third rifle that cracked through the night — exploding a bullet that hit the Japanese in the left thigh. The impact half turned the man before he started to topple. His finger tugged at the trigger and the shot tore uselessly through the wall of fire.

Edge took aim at the falling form and squeezed his trigger a second time. The wounded Japanese went down faster than he anticipated and the bullet entered his head, to exit through the top of the skull trailed by a splash of blood, tissue and bone fragments. The dead man dropped his rifle and went from sight, sliding down the slope in the wake of his partner.

'Edge *san*.' a voice called shrilly. 'Are they finished?'

'They're sure over the hill,' the half-breed growled: and rolled on to his back, narrowed eyes under the hooded lids searching for the source of the shouted words. Right hand pumping the lever action of the Winchester to ready another bullet should it be needed.

But the man who had probably saved his life was not about to try to take it. He stood on the seat of the flatbed wagon which was parked on the western ridge of the valley. A short, slimly built man with his rifle held in both hands, but slung low across the middle of his thighs. A man dressed Western style but who spoke American with a similar accent to the Japanese.

Edge used his rifle simply to beckon the man to come down into the valley. Then sat up and turned to look at Ralph. As he had rolled over to search for the newcomer, he was aware that the barrel of the Winchester knocked off Ralph's hat. Now he saw it was not just the hat which was displaced. The hold-up man's head had rolled, too: revealing the ghastly wound where one of the Oriental's curved swords had sliced powerfully through the neck. The blood had not quite congealed: was still tacky as it began to change colour from sheened red to matt black.

'Them or me, feller,' Edge muttered as he drew the blankets off the headless torso of Ralph. 'Ever since Olsen Creek you were bound to come to a sticky end.'

CHAPTER TEN

RALPH had no money in his pockets so, as the fire began to burn out from lack of fuel in the south and the stranger brought the wagon carefully down the grassy slope, Edge went in search of the dead Japanese. He found their crumpled, blood-spattered bodies just a few yards below the hill crest. Both had died with their eyes open and their sightless stares rebuked him as he delved through the brightly coloured robes. Nothing.

He continued on down into the hollow and found what he was looking for in a saddlebag — the money and Silas Martin's gold watch wrapped and tied in a brown paper package. In the same saddlebag was a pair of powerful fieldglasses. But he took only what belonged to him and the old man, then untied the hobbles on the horses and back-tracked over the rise to Ralph's camp.

The wagon was down in the valley by then, the stranger still sitting hunched on the seat, staring fixedly at the severed head of Ralph lying on its side three feet from the gruesome patch of gore between the shoulders.

'Obliged to you, kid,' Edge said, his greeting startling the Oriental youngster out of his private world of horror.

'It was less than nothing, Edge *san*. I aimed to kill the man and failed.'

Then he gave a strangled cry, leapt down off the wagon and fell on to all fours. A torrent of dull coloured vomit gushed from his open mouth to form a pool between his hands.

Edge used a booted foot to drag the displaced head close to the torso, then draped a blanket over the remains of Ralph before he went to the rear of the flatbed to check on Silas Martin. A saddled horse hitched to the wagon's tailgate looked dolefully at the half-breed.

'He breathes still, but he is very weak I think,' the stranger

101

said as he rose unsteadily to his feet, using the back of a hand to wipe the stains of nausea off his chin.

Edge thought that the dusty, bristled face of Martin showed no change from the last time he had looked at it.

'You want to tell me about you, kid?' he asked as he moved to crouch down beside the gelding which had lost its rider at the Olsen Creek Union Pacific halt.

The animal was calm now that the flames had died and the taint of smoke had disappeared from the air. It lay still, close to exhaustion from its struggles, as the half-breed released it from its hobble.

'My name is Yoshio. Americans call me Shio. I am friend of Martin *san*.'

Edge gently stroked the neck of the gelding, then eased carefully away. The horse had to make three attempts before he was able to stand up. He took a few steps and seemed in danger of collapsing. But then he stretched his neck down and began to crop at a patch of grass.

'But it ain't a small world,' the half-breed responded after he was sure the gelding had recovered.

'*San*?'

'It was no accident you ran into him out here in nowhere.' He went to the saddles, to reclaim his own Winchester and retrieve the Remington and Martin's tiny gun from one of the bags.

'No, Edge *san*. I have been searching for him.'

The half-breed climbed up on to the wagon seat and beckoned for the youthful Japanese to join him: and as the boy approached he looked at him closely for the first time.

He was little more than five feet tall and probably did not weigh in excess of a hundred and ten pounds. He was handsome, almost pretty in immaturity, with a clear, smooth skin which looked as if it had never felt the scrape of a razor. His complexion was sallow, his slitted eyes brown and his lips full and very red. He was aged somewhere between fifteen and twenty.

He moved with a strange awkwardness for such a slimly

built youngster — almost as if he made a conscious effort to inject stiffness into a frame that was naturally loose limbed. He was dressed in black Levi's, a grey shirt, red kerchief, black Stetson and spurred black riding boots. A gunbelt encircled his small waist, with a Frontier Colt in a holster on the right hip. All his clothes — and even the revolver — seemed slightly too large for him.

'Since when?' Edge asked as he flicked the reins and released the brake lever to set the flatbed rolling — south along the bottom of the valley.

'Since he returned to this country from the land of my ancestors, Edge *san*.'

'Why?'

'Because I knew he needed help and he once helped me. Saved my life when I was ...'

'That's bullshit, Edge!' Silas Martin snarled. 'Kill the little ...'

The rage of frustration in helplessness gave the dying old man the strength to shout the denial and demand very loudly The words, yelled by a man they both thought was locked in unconsciousness startled the half-breed and the Oriental.

Edge recovered first, but had both hands on the reins. His reflexes were additionally slowed by the suspicion that Silas Martin might not be aware of what he was saying — had yelled in delirium as he came half awake from a terrifying nightmare.

But as he turned his head to look back at the old man, he saw the handsome face of Shio become ugly with a sneer. And the way the boy's shoulder rose warned the half-breed he was reaching for his gun.

It was the boy's shrill shriek of alarm that cut across Martin's order and silenced it. The cry vented as Edge slid forcefully along the seat, to crash his hip against that of Shio. The weight and power behind the impact sent the boy hard against the handrail at the end of the seat. He had his gun clear of the holster by then, but dropped it as he clawed with both hands to grip the handrail. He missed and the momentum of

103

the slide across the seat canted his head and torso out over the side of the wagon.

The pain of his hip hitting the handrail altered the tone of his cry. Then fear was the stronger emotion again as Edge hooked a hand under his rump and heaved. Shio was lifted up off the seat and sent sailing over the side of the flatbed, arms and legs beating at thin air. He hit the ground hard, face down: but with his wits still about him. The Colt was resting just six inches from his outstretched right hand. He clawed his fingers to dig them into the dusty ground and haul himself within reach.

The half-breed released the reins, dragged the lever over to lock the brake blocks to the wheel rims, and leaned over the handrail to aim his Remington. The recoil of the shot juddered the bones from his knuckles to his elbow. Shio screamed what sounded like a foreign language obscenity and snatched his right hand away from the bullet hole in the ground beside the Colt.

'A life for a life,' Edge said evenly. 'I'm no longer beholden to you. So there's no future in trying for the gun. For you, miss.'

'Miss!' the youthful looking Japanese gasped. 'How did you . . .'

'Kill her, Edge!' Silas Martin snarled, the power gone from his voice. He moaned with pain. 'Kill the little whore!'

'You didn't get down there on your own,' the half-breed reminded the girl and raised his left hand as he curled back his lips in a cold grin. 'I gave you a hand and didn't feel a thing.'

She bent her knees and arched her back to rise on to all fours, withdrawing her hand from the Colt. Then she got to her feet. As she dusted off her pants and shirt her actions were no longer stiffly awkward: there was a natural feminine fluidity to her movements now that the charade was over.

'He is paying you,' she said with a nod toward the rear of the wagon, and even her voice was different now. 'Why do you not do as he orders and kill me?'

Edge straightened up on the seat and slid the Remington

back into its holster. 'For five dollars a day I'll listen to the word from my sponsor, lady. But I direct the shots.'

'She's no lady!' Martin rasped. 'She's a five dollar whore out of the Devil's Acre in Frisco.'

'So she rates higher than me, feller. I'm working twenty-four hours a day for that money. You want to get back up on the wagon, Shio? I guess that isn't your name, though?'

'My name is Sui Lin.'

Edge jerked a thumb over his shoulder. 'Any relation to the corpse?'

'We are ... were sisters.'

'Don't listen to her, Edge,' the dying man ordered, then altered his tone to that of pleading. 'She's no better than Hitoshi and his men. She wants to rob me. All whores are liars and cheats. She'll tell you a pack of lies, son.'

Sui Lin did not move while Martin was abusing her with his tongue. Simply stood and gazed mournfully up at the half-breed.

'I said do you want to get back on the wagon?' he told her.

'Damn you, Edge!' the old man snarled as the wagon springs creaked softly under the meagre weight of the girl climbing aboard.

'Thank you, Edge *san*,' Sui Lin said with a sigh as she sat gratefully down, took off her hat and shook her head so that her sheened black hair tumbled down to reach below her shoulders at front and back. 'But you should know he speaks the truth. I am a whore and it was my plan to lie to you and rob him.'

The half-breed had rolled a cigarette. Now he lit it, released the brake lever and took up the reins to urge the team into movement. 'Never have held anything against whores,' he said. 'And if liars and cheats bothered me I figure I wouldn't be able to get along with anybody.'

'You wish me to tell you my story now, Edge *san*?'

'It sure as hell ain't your willing body that interests me,' he growled. 'So forget you're a whore.'

She turned her Orientally pretty face toward his hard set profile marked with countless cuts and grazes from the thorns, her almond shaped eyes puzzled.

'I want to hear the truth, girl. Don't try to screw me.'

CHAPTER ELEVEN

SILAS MARTIN passed out before the girl's story was half told, soon after Edge had halted the wagon and lit a cooking fire about three miles south east of the valley.

The camp site he chose was in a gully on the southern fringe of the group of hills, sheltered from the breeze which blew stronger and colder as the night progressed. They had tried to lift the old man down from the wagon, but the pain was too much for him to take: and when he stopped screaming and plunged deep beneath the level of consciousness, they left him where he lay: grey faced and his chest hardly rising and falling at all.

When a pan of water had been boiled, Edge made to bathe the stinking bullet wound and apply a fresh dressing. But the girl, whose sex was emphasised by the action of the wind in contouring the loose fitting shirt to the sparse curves of her breasts, insisted on undertaking the chore.

'He was good to us once,' she said as Edge leaned over the side of the wagon to check that she meant Martin no harm. 'And is there anything I can do to make it worse for him, *san*?'

'No sweat,' the half-breed muttered, his glinting eyes glancing once more at the withered, lined flesh of the once full-faced Silas Martin. 'He dies now or a week from now, I don't figure he'll wake up again.'

'But he remained conscious for long enough for you to believe me?'

Edge did not reply. Simply turned and went to the fire, to sit on her saddle, drink fresh made coffee and consider what Sui Lin had told him.

'Mai Lin and I were whores. We worked in a house on Kearney Street. As he said, in that part of San Francisco known as the Devil's Acre. What he did not say is that he owned the house. And Mai Lin and me and the other girls.'

'You want to say anything now, Silas?' Edge had asked.

'Nothin' you'd want to hear. Let her talk.' His voice had been very weak. Little more than a strained whisper — as if his agony had formed a hard ball in his throat and he had to squeeze the words out around it.

'Several weeks ago, a seaman came to the house and chose Mai Lin. He was very drunk. When he learned I was sister to Mai Lin, he wanted both of us. Which was not strange, and he had money to pay. But while we were doing what he demanded, another man came. There was a fight. With knives. Both men were badly wounded. Mai Lin too. But accident, when knife is thrown and misses man, hit her. I was afraid and ran to bring Martin *san*. When we get back to room Mai Lin is dead. So is the man who began fight — an Italian. Martin *san* sent me away, says he will do what is necessary to keep lawmen from coming to house.'

The girl spoke without any trace of emotion, sitting easily on the seat, riding with the pitch and roll and jolt of the wagon while her gaze was directed straight ahead between the heads of the two horses.

'I never see him again until tonight.'

'And it must have given you a big kick, finding me shot almost into hell,' Martin rasped. 'Why didn't you just finish me off, girl?'

'It did not suit my purpose. And I am not a murderer, Martin *san*. I have never tried to harm anyone until I shot Hitoshi tonight.'

'That gave you the taste,' Edge put in.

She sighed. 'I was angry and afraid. I do not know if I could have shot you. If I had, I would be very sorry.'

'Been a little upset myself,' Edge muttered. 'What happened after the killings at the house?'

'I waited for the rest of the night in my room. With grief for Mai Lin and fear for myself. Then men came. In the morning. Hitoshi, Zenko and Toru.'

'Who weren't no Samuria warriors, I figure,' Edge growled.

'I sold you a bill of goods, son,' Martin admitted, using words and expressions he had never spoken while maintaining his pretence of being the wandering black sheep of a rich eastern family. 'A man who runs a whore house in a seaport city can't help learning a lot about exotic places. I didn't trust a man like you to know the truth. Jesus, I feel ill.'

'I ain't feeling too good either, feller.'

Martin managed to rise momentarily above his misery. 'Makes an old man very happy to hear that.'

'So maybe you'll die with a smile on your face,' the half-breed rasped, and immediately regretted it.

Silas Martin had never had very long left to live: and just one dream left to live for. A stroke of good fortune had caused him to ignite a spark of feeling in the cold heart of Edge — when he had claimed Mai Lin as his wife. With no way of knowing that this lie left the normally cynical and sceptical half-breed wide open to swallow a whole lot more. So, Edge acknowledged, as he halted the wagon in the gully where he intended to make night camp, he had only himself — the way he was — to blame for the situation he was in.

'I think you are right, Edge *san*,' Sui Lin said sadly as she came to sit down beside him at the fire. 'He will die without waking.'

The food and cooking pots were nearby and she began to prepare a stew.

'Which means he won't be able to confirm the rest of what you have to tell me,' the half-breed pointed out flatly.

'Do the words matter? In the coffin of Mai Lin is the reason for all that has happened. You can open it at any time and see for yourself.'

'I've seen enough dead people for one day. You want to tell me what I've been killing them for?'

'A golden Buddha from the Orient, Edge *san*. Solid gold and studded with precious gems. Stolen from a holy temple in Cathay and brought to this country by the seaman who died in Mai Lin's room at the house of Martin *san*.

The half-breed's lack of expression in the light of the moon and flickering fire was a true sign of his feelings at the revelation. Ever since he had learned that the corpse in the coffin meant nothing to the old man, it had followed that money or the means to get money was the real reason for Martin's journey.

'Worth how much?'

'In the land from which it came, it is priceless. Here, the metal and jewels could not be purchased for less than half a million dollars.'

Sui Lin waited for a question which did not come. Then answered the one she had expected. 'Hitoshi told me this. He and Zenko and Toru were well known in San Francisco. They worked for very rich Japanese who has many houses. Many saloons. Places for glambling. Hitoshi told me man who brought Golden Buddha from Cathay had promised to sell it to this rich man. One who started fight worked for another rich man. Seaman dead by then. Not from knife wound, though. Strangled. And Martin *san* gone. Body of Mai Lin, too. And Golden Buddha from bag of seaman. Gone many hours before Hitoshi and others find seaman had come to house of Martin *san*.'

She had finished preparing the food and set it to cook in the pot. She asked with her eyes if she was allowed to pour herself a mug of coffee and the half-breed nodded his permission. She blew on the steaming black liquid and took several sips before she continued.

'It did not surprise me, what Martin *san* had done. All the time he used to talk of making much money to enjoy when he was old man. I think of this after Hitoshi and others leave me. And I remember how he talked of going back to his birthplace. In New York City where he was very poor. He spoke of how good it would be to be rich in New York City.'

'You didn't tell Hitoshi about that?' Edge asked as the breeze snatched at the steam from the cooking pot and wafted its appetising aroma across his nostrils.

'No, *san*. I did not think of such things until later. And then

110

I began to think that I should share in the good fortune of Martin *san*. And I will not lie to you by saying it was because my sister died. I thought only of myself.'

'Thinking of the dead you can get to be one of them,' the half-breed said sourly, reflecting on the number of times he had almost died since a memory of Beth had aroused his misplaced sympathy for Silas Martin.

'I do not understand, Edge *san*,' Sui Lin responded, confused.

'As long as I do.' He showed her a bleak expression, his gaze much colder than the strengthening wind which was starting to make moaning sounds through the hills to the north.

She shivered, not from the chill of the night. 'You hate me very much, I think, Edge *san*.'

'You and me are in the human race,' he rasped bitterly. 'Nothing makes us different from the rest.'

She stirred the stew while she considered this, then decided there was no point in projecting her thoughts about it any further. 'You wish to know the rest?'

'Your voice sounds sweeeter than the one in my head.'

Again she chose to ignore the cryptic self-directed bitterness of the impassive man and lay back on the grass. She pulled a blanket over her body and stared up at the stars with her hands linked behind her head.

'I started out for New York City, Edge *san*. Dressed as a boy because I thought it would be easier for me to travel so. I had only enough money to buy a ticket on the railroad to Kansas City but I knew I would be able to earn more there. Or anywhere.'

'Except here with me.'

She showed anger for the first time since he had tipped her off the wagon at Ralph's camp. 'I do not care that you do not need whores! Many others do!'

The half-breed glanced down at her face which showed above the blanket and, because she refused to look at him, felt free to briefly display his feelings on his thorn-torn face. As was so often the case with pretty girls and beautiful women, she looked more desirable than ever with the light of anger in her eyes and petulence forming the set of her lips. But he could not desire her because she was a whore. And what ran through his mind was regret that he could not want her — and the many others of her kind he had met during his aimless drifting since the end of the war. For if he could have used whores he would have avoided much heartache. For him there would have been no Beth Day, no Emma Diamond, no Charity Meagher, no Isabella Montez. Before the end of the war, no Jeannie Fisher. Women loved and lost, all but one of them violently. The losing of them always having some traumatic effect on him which motivated his later actions.

He shook his head to clear his mind of futile reflections on the unchangeable past. And considered asking Sui Lin if she knew how big a city was New York and how she planned on finding one man among so many. But now, that was immaterial, too. Just as he had given little thought to the circumstances in which he had met up again with Hitoshi and Zenko.

The field glasses in the saddlebag had given the clue. Out on the mid-western prairie it had been easy for them to stay ahead of their quarry, beyond the range of the human eye which had no artificial magnifying lens to aid it: paying others to risk their lives and then taking the life of a man to set a trap in a situation that looked safe.

'The train got only as far as Denver before the snow came,' the Japanese whore went on, after time and the lack of response from Edge had soothed her rancour. 'I saw Martin *san* come into town a few days later with the box on the wagon. But he had men to guard it and law officers were involved. So I waited and watched. I was at the railroad station when Hitoshi and the others tried to steal the box in which I knew the Golden Buddha had to be. I saw you kill Toru.'

'I didn't owe him anything any more.'

'Like me now.'

'Won't have any reason to kill you if you don't aim a gun at me again.'

She sat up. 'What about the Golden Buddha?'

'Sometimes I have to kill people. Never do steal from them.'

The girl looked at him with a cynical expression, not believing his indfference toward the valuable religious relic. But the hardness in his slitted eyes, glinting like chips of blue metal in a match flare as he lit a cigarette, drove her gaze away from his face. She stirred the stew, even though it was unnecessary.

'What are you going to do, Edge *san*?'

'My job. Was hired to guard the casket from Denver to New York state.'

'By a man who lied to you. A man who will die soon.'

The half-breed nodded. 'The way he is now, there's nothing I can do about the lies. When he cashes in, my job'll be over.'

'And if I am with you?' There was excitement in her voice.

'Finish your story, girl.'

She had to take time to collect her thoughts — recall the point at which she had broken off. Her face continued to glow with the fervent expectation that the means to a fortune hidden in the casket was destined to come to her.

'I left Denver on the second passenger train, certain a man such as you would get the Golden Buddha safely to New York City. But the train broke down at the station beyond Olsen Creek. While we waited for another locomotive, a freight train came. And I heard talk of the two Orientals who held the brakeman prisoner until Butcherville. I was afraid for you and Martin *san* ...' She looked at him for a moment and shrugged. 'For the Golden Buddha. I did not have enough money to buy a horse, so I stole one. At Olsen Creek I found the dead man and saw horse and wheel tracks. I followed them. When I came upon the wagon with Martin *san* in it I tried to rouse him. But he would not revive. So I hitched the horses and began to drive the wagon. I did not know where I was going until I saw the glow of the fire you lit. That is all there is to tell you, Edge *san*.

She reached for two plates and began to ladle the food from the pot, heaping more on the half-breed's than her own.

'Except for why you shot Hitoshi or Zenko or whoever he was. But I guess I know that already.'

113

She gave him his plate. 'He would have come looking for wagon and killed me for having the Golden Buddha. I knew nothing of what you would do. So I took chance.'

'Food's good.'

'I always cooked for Martin *san* and girls of house. Did I take right chance, Edge *san*?'

'I figure you did, but I'm prejudiced.'

'What you going to do?'

'I told you. My job.'

'I can come with you?'

'If you can afford it. Aim to get to Cimarron and pick up an A.T. and S.F. train eastbound. Need to buy tickets.'

'I can sell horse and saddle. Nobody there will know I stole them.'

'If they do, they'll hang you.'

'For Golden Buddha, I will take another chance.'

They ate in silence for several minutes. Then Sui Lin said: 'When we have finished, I will bathe your face, Edge *san*. You suffered many cuts in overcoming trap of Hitoshi and Zenko. I saw you fall two times and was fearful they would get to top of hill before you got to gun at bottom. I am very glad you win race.'

The half-breed ran the tips of his fingers over his blood encrusted features. The tears in the skin no longer pained him but after sitting so long by the fire his legs had started to ache when he made any small movement: protesting the effects of the unusual exertion when he had chased the train at Butcherville and hurtled down toward Ralph's camp.

'Yeah,' he muttered with a grimace. 'I didn't do so bad for a scratch runner.'

CHAPTER TWELVE

NEWS of the trouble on the Union Pacific railroad had not reached the cow town of Cimarron which was on the Atchison, Topeka and Santa Fe line. The local doctor looked at Silas Martin, said there was nothing he could do for the old man — who should be dead anyway — and sold Edge some salve and clean dressings to put on the stinking, pus-inflamed bullet hole. The fee for this was eight dollars and the half-breed took money from Martin's stake to pay it.

Sui Lin, dressed like a man but making no pretence of being one, managed to get a good price for the stolen horse and gear in time to buy a ticket and join the first eastbound train to leave town.

She and Edge rode in a day car after installing the old man in a sleeper berth, where he would be able to live out the final remnants of his now useless life, unaware of the relative comfort he was enjoying. He was the only occupant of his car, so there was nobody to be bothered by the rancid smell of his rotting flesh.

The casket was in the caboose, the cheerful brakeman blissfully ignorant of what the crate contained.

At hourly intervals during the days and nights, as the train rattled and swayed from Cimarron to Dodge City, Dodge to Wichita, to Newton, to Topeka, either the girl or the half-breed checked on Martin's condition. Each time they were certain that on the next occasion they looked, he would be dead.

Although he was sure Sui Lin had neither the inclination nor the courage to help Silas Martin out of this life, he guessed that she was willing him to die: was eager for the stage to be reached when her travelling companion had to make known his intention for the Golden Buddha.

115

Edge himself waited stoically for nature and the ingenuity of avaricious men to take their courses. For two things were certain. The old man would die. And the men of wealth who sought to enrich themselves further would not allow a Devil's Acre whore to steal the Golden Buddha. Which reduced it to a matter of time.

Would Silas Martin die soon so that the half-breed could take what he was owed and leave? Or would he continue to cling to the slender thread of his life for long enough for Edge to be present at the end of a contest — a race between the man for whom the trio of Japanese had worked, and the one who had sent the Italian to Martin's cat house. The former had reason to want Edge dead, in revenge for the killing of Hitoshi, Zenko and Toru. The latter? If the old man were still breathing, the half-breed's code would demand that he continue to guard the crated casket.

The man who won the race had his guns waiting at the station of a small town a few miles south west of the Kansas River crossing beyond Topeka.

The train clanked to a halt alongside the depot boardwalk as the hands on the clock above the door of the despatcher's office showed the time of three o'clock in the morning.

Edge was awake, smoking a cigarette as a prelude to heading back into the next car to check on the pitifully wasted and weak Silas Martin. The girl at his side slept on, merely venting a low groan as the halting of the train caused her chin to fall forward on to her chest.

The moon was bright in a clear sky above eastern Kansas, showing a boardwalk deserted except for a railman standing beside a pile of cartons and sacks outside the despatcher's office.

The dozen or so other passengers in the car continued to sleep as peacefully as the Japanese girl, even when the man on the boardwalk yelled at the brakeman to come and help him load the freight.

Edge rose from his window seat and instinctively picked

up his Winchester before he swung over the legs of Sui Lin and started down the unlit car. When he stepped out on to the railed platform, a man said:

'You gotta be the one, I guess.'

He and another man were down on the right, on the other side of the train from the boardwalk. Both dressed in sombre hued city suits and both aiming Frontier Colts at the half-breed. Swathy-skinned, big built men with eyes like dark pebbles.

'The one what?' Edge countered, his right hand hanging lower than his holster and his left wrapped around the frame of the rifle which was canted to his shoulder.

'The one that either acts sensible or gets dead,' the second man responded, speaking with the same Latin style accent as the first.

'We heard about you from Newton. By telegraph. Our man told us what Martin's man looked like.'

'You wanna toss down your guns? Or you wanna look a little different? With a hole in you you don't have now.'

'Mr Marlon ain't bothered, one way or the other.'

'I ain't of the same opinion as Mr Marlon,' Edge said, and made to bring the Winchester gently down from his shoulder.

But the leading door of the sleeper car opened and a third city-suited man stepped through. He looked to be of the same southern European nationality as the two on the ground and was in the same mid-thirties age group. He was not surprised to see the half-breed.

'I'll take it,' he said, reaching out over the two rails and easing the rifle from Edge's grasp. 'And if you don't turn to the side so I can get your handgun, you're dead. Mr Marlon . . .'

'I already know how he feels about me, feller.' He swung his right hip toward the man on the other car and allowed the Remington to be slid out of the holster.

'Martin didn't oughta be alive,' the third man told his partners. 'He won't cause no trouble.'

'What about the whore?'

The man with Edge's guns looked quizzically at their owner.

117

A brown skinned thumb was hooked and stabbed over a broad shoulder.

'Asleep.'

'Go wake her up and bring her out here, Rico.' Then to Edge: 'You, get down on the boardwalk. Keep playing it right and you get to be in a thousand bucks. Play it wrong and you get to be out of breath. You know what I mean?'

A fourth man appeared on the boardwalk side of the train. Another Italian, dressed in a black derby, black suit, white shirt, black tie and black patent leather shoes. Holding a Frontier Colt in his right fist.

'That Mr Marlon is giving me a message it's hard to refuse,' the half-breed muttered and stepped down from the train.

'That's where you head for,' the fourth smartly turned out gunman instructed as Edge looked toward the rear of the train. Where yet another man held a gun, aimed at the brakeman and despatcher, while two others sweated and struggled to move the crated casket out of the caboose.

As he started forward, the half-breed glanced over his shoulder. There was no one in sight beside the locomotive, but he guessed one of Marlon's men was in the cabin, covering the footplate crew.

'For a hick Western gunslinger you did all right against Boss Black's Frisco boys,' the man behind Edge growled.

'Not so hot against you fellers.'

'Some you win, some you lose. With us, least you got the choice if you want to live or die.'

'No contest.'

Other footfalls rapped on the boardwalk and Edge glanced back again: saw Rico and the other two suited men urging the sullen looking Sui Lin to hurry ahead of them.

At the rear of the train, the heavy crate was finally lowered to the boardwalk beside the caboose. All the gunmen glanced toward the man with Edge's Winchester and Remington as he joined the loose knit group around the crate. This man stabbed a finger at the sweating, lip-quivering despatcher.

'You get aboard with the brakeman. Tell both of you what's

been told the engineer. The train don't stop until it reaches Kansas City. Raise any kind of alarm you want then. Okay?'

Both railmen nodded and moved hurriedly around the crate to reach the caboose.

'Ain't okay with me,' Edge said, and drew every pair of eyes towards him.

The railmen's fear expanded as they froze in the act of climbing up into the caboose. Sui Lin looked morose in defeat. The gunmen expressed tacit snarls.

'If I'm staying,' he went on, 'I'd like for the old man to get off here, too.'

'You're in no position to want anything, except stay alive,' the leader of the gunmen snapped.

'Buy the favour for the thousand dollars you planned to pay me, feller.'

'Why?'

'I'm working for him. He could wake up before he dies. Like for him to see I didn't run out on him.'

'We can't spare the time for that kinda crap, Louie!' the man behind Edge rasped.

'Shuddup,' he was told by the frowning Louie, who then nodded. His forefinger stabbed toward the brakeman and despatcher. 'You guys get aboard further up the train. Rico, unhook the last car and caboose from the train. Emilio and Carlo, start opening the crate.' He glanced at Edge, and aimed the Winchester at him. 'Sentiment like that, I got feelings for. But you try to pull anything, you'll die ahead of the old guy.'

'I still know what you mean, feller.'

As soon as the brakeman and despatcher were aboard, Rico came out from uncoupling the sleeper car and caboose from the last day car. He put a finger and thumb in his mouth and vented a shrill whistle that pierced through the hiss of escaping steam. A man climbed down from the locomotive, gestured with his gun hand and was shrouded with billowing grey vapour. Drive wheels spun and then gripped the track. The cars jolted forward, clashing bumpers, then began to roll smoothly as they gathered speed under the powerful thrust of the locomotive.

Crowbars prised the top off the crate with a teeth-gritting sound of nails forced out from timber. All of Marlon's men, with the exception of the two opening the crate and Louie who kept Edge and Sui Lin covered with the Winchester, went from sight beyond the depot building.

Smoke from the departing train drifted across the boardwalk, not thick enough to hide anything from anyone.

'She's been dead a long time, you guys,' Louie warned as the top of the crate was removed and they started to unscrew the casket lid.

The two men interrupted their chore to take the white linen handkerchiefs from the breast pockets of their jackets. They tied them at the napes of their necks to form masks over their mouths and noses.

'Please treat Mai Lin with respect,' Sui Lin asked dully. 'She was my sister.'

'I didn't know that,' Louie said, mildly surprised.

'Only God knows everything, *san*.'

Louie showed very white teeth in a confident smile. 'A lot of people in New York think Mr Marlon is God, sister. He always knows enough.'

The sounds from the train had been swallowed up by the night and the tiny, unlit town behind the depot would have been silent had not a wagon begun to roll.

Edge turned from peering across the track at an expanse of cottonwoods with a trail curving into it and watched a Concord coach hauled by four geldings. With Rico controlling the reins and Carlo sitting on the high seat beside him, the Concord moved slowly along the street beside the boardwalk, then made a sharp turn to go over the timber crossing and halt at the start of the trail. The balance of Marlon's men stared dead-pan out of the windows.

'*Mamma mia!*'

'*Dio! Il fetore!*'

The lid of the casket slid from the hands of the man who

120

had removed it and clattered to the boardwalk. He and his partner both staggered back, using their hands to supplement the handkerchief masks over their lower faces.

Then the nauseatingly sweet stench of long decayed flesh permeated through the warm, early hours air to assault the nostrils of Edge, Sui Lin and Louie. The girl and the Italian stepped back: as the half-breed moved forward, once more recalling a vivid image of Beth. She had not been dead so long when he found her, but her maggot infested remains had smelled as bad.

Nature had started to strip the flesh from the bones of Mai Lin. Already her eyes were gone, her nose was half eaten away and probably she had no tongue in her mouth, which was filled with tiny worms, writhing and twisting as they continued to feed.

'It there?' Louie called.

Edge glanced over his shoulder to where the Italian continued to keep him covered with his own Winchester. 'If it was that easy to find, Martin wouldn't have got it past the Denver law, feller.'

'Marco! Franco! Finish your job!'

The two men looked about to refuse, but the glare in Louie's eyes froze the words in their throats. They advanced tentatively to the other side of the crated casket from Edge. Then, after a moment's hesitation, began to delve their hands under the white satin shroud which clothed the corpse, their heads averted to try to escape the worst of the stench.

Edge watched them for a few seconds, then reached into the coffin, hooked curled fingers under the neckline of the shroud, and jerked his arm.

Marco and Franco vented cries of fear through their masks and stumbled backward.

'What the hell?' Louie demanded, as alarmed as his men by the half-breed's sudden move.

Even Rico and Carlo snatched up their Colts from the Concord seat and swung them to aim at Edge.

'When a job stinks, best way to do it is fast, feller.'

The maggots had feasted on the hirsute base of Mai Lin's belly and like those crawling in her mouth they did not interrupt their gorging on the rotted tissue.

Edge's narrowed eyes raked the nude body from neck to crotch and rasped through compressed lips: 'Just to use on her,' as he drew the razor from its neck pouch.

The knife which had killed the Japanese whore went in under her sparse left breast. Perhaps had been ripped upward, or maybe the cut had been made later. She had obviously been dead when the inexpert stitches were used to pull the two flaps of flesh together. The strong thread was partially rotted, and parted easily under the attack of the finely honed blade.

The half-breed wiped the blade on the shroud and pushed it back into the pouch.

Horrified fascination emanated from every pair of eyes which watched him stoop, pick up the discarded screwdrivers and lean over the open casket again.

Only he was in a position to see the skin of the whore's breast fragment like scorched paper as he used the screwdrivers to scrape it away. And so he was the first to see the jewel studded statuette of the grinning, swollen-bellied Buddha which had been pressed into the cavity where Mai Lin's heart had once been.

He looked at the sculptured gold and finely cut gems bleakly for a few moments. Then dropped the tools in the casket and stepped back from the crate.

'You have it?' Louie asked hoarsely.

'Found the gold, but it ain't mine. Like to go check on Silas now.'

'*Momento!*' the Italian snapped, and addressed a burst of words in his own language at Franco.

Marco expressed relief as he retreated to the Concord, taking the handkerchief from his face. The sick looking Franco also removed his mask, to protect his hands from the touch of decayed flesh, as he delved into the mutilated body and lifted out the Golden Buddha.

Men gasped as gold, diamonds, rubies and emeralds glistened and glinted in the moonlight.

Sui Lin vented a moan of despair.

Edge turned and started along the boardwalk toward the rear of the sleeper car.

'*Signore!*' Louie called after him, causing the half-breed to halt and look back.

'Yeah, feller?'

'You should know that Mr Marlon was offered the statue first. He was willing to pay a fair price. The others tried to steal it.'

Edge did not reply. Simply continued on his way to the sleeper car, as Louie and Franco went toward the Concord coach. Sui Lin cupped both hands over her mouth and nose as she moved nervously up to the crate to peer in at the ghastly remains of her sister.

Once aboard the car, the half-breed lengthened his stride to reach the berth where the old man lay. He jerked the drape curtain aside and delved under the blankets to bring out Sui Lin's Winchester and Martin's tiny revolver before he even looked at the old man's face.

In the moonlight shafting through the car window, the heavily bristled flesh looked the same colour as that of the corpse outside. The hairs growing from Martin's nostrils wavered fractionally as air sucked in through the parted lips was expelled through the nose.

'You sure are making me work for my money, you old bastard,' Edge growled as he heard a shout and then the clop of hooves and creak of timbers as the Concord rolled forward.

'Edge *san!*' Sui Lin called desperately as she entered the sleeper through the rear door. 'What can we do against so many?'

'Our best,' the half-breed responded, and tossed the My Friend revolver toward her.

She failed to catch the gun and stooped to pick it up from the floor.

'It'll make a noise is all,' he told her as he leaned over an unmade berth across the aisle from where Silas Martin was dying. And crashed the muzzle of the Winchester against the window to shower shattered glass on to the track side.

The Concord was almost into the cottonwoods by then, but still close enough to the depot for the men aboard to hear the smash.

Both Carlo and Rico whirled to look back, and Edge used his first bullet on the man with the reins: seeing blood spurt from the centre of a face carved with shock.

Rico started to turn the other way, then pitched forward, off the seat to go down between the two nearest horses.

Another shot exploded as the half-breed pumped the lever action of the repeater. Louder than a report from the My Friend or any of the Colts carried by Marlon's men.

Perhaps from Edge's Winchester which Louie had taken with him?

But it was Carlo who took the bullet, screaming as he tumbled over the side of the stage coach.

The team made to bolt in reaction to the shots and falling bodies. But then dropped dead in their traces as a violent fusillade of rifle fire filled the warm night air on the north fringe of the small Kansas town.

Muzzle flashes stabbed out of the cottonwoods to either side of the stalled Concord. And Edge stayed his curled forefinger on the trigger of the Winchester as he heard the smashing of glass, the screams and curses of trapped men and the continuous barrage of gunfire.

Then came stretched seconds of utter silence.

He shifted his gaze away from the bullet-scarred Concord to peer into the darkness of the trees, swinging his rifle first one way and then the other. It was so quiet that he could hear the steady drip of dead men's blood as the droplets fell from the cracks at the base of the coach doors.

'Edge *san*, what . . .'

Sui Lin's tense spoken query was curtailed by another burst of rifle fire. And Edge threw himself down into the aisle as a dozen bullets smashed through windows or tore into the timber sides of the sleeper car. He peered along the dusty boards as another volley of bullets was triggered from the cottonwoods and saw that the girl was also on the floor. A dark stain slowly expanded its area from beneath the side of her head pressed to the boards.

'Whore ought to have the sense to know when to go down,' he muttered and eased up on to his haunches to look into Martin's berth.

The hairs in the old man's nose no longer moved. When the half-breed delved a hand under the blankets, he failed to locate any rise and fall of the chest.

'You cashed in at the right time, Silas,' he said as he drew the old man's money from a jacket pocket. 'Now it's my turn.'

He took what was owed and replaced the balance of the money. Only then turned to look through the smashed window toward the cottonwoods. In time to see the shadowy figure of a man step from the bullet riddled, corpse laden Concord, clutching to his chest something which seemed to catch fire when the moonlight briefly struck it.

'Guess Marlon didn't know about you fellers,' he rasped.

Then the man was gone, swallowed by the blackness among the trees. Other footfalls sounded in the timber. Silence again for a while. Next the thud of hooves as many horses were urged to a gallop. This sound soon fading into nothingness.

Edge left the bodies of Silas Martin and Sui Lin aboard the sleeper without looking at them again, and stepped down on to the boardwalk. He held the Winchester in the crook of his arm as he leaned against the side of the caboose, dug out the makings and rolled a cigarette.

The warm night air neutralised the acrid taint of drifting gunsmoke. But the stench of Mai Lin's decomposed flesh was as strong as ever.

Lights began to show at windows and doorways in the small town. And before he had smoked his cigarette a small group of the more adventurous citizens had come on to the street which ran alongside the boardwalk. They were hurriedly dressed, their faces heavy and their hair tousled from sleep.

They came to an abrupt halt, grimacing as they caught the cloyingly sweet smell from the open crate.

'Hey, mister!' a man called fearfully. 'What was all the shooting for?'

'And for God's sake, what's makin' that stink?' somebody else demanded hoarsely.

The whole group backed away a pace as the half-breed moved his rifle: but only to cant it to his left shoulder. Then he straightened up from the side of the caboose and flicked the stub of the cigarette down on to the track.

'Same answer to both questions,' he said evenly, his lean features almost completely shadowed by the brim of his hat as he moved between the crate and the caboose and stepped off the boardwalk heading for the ambushed Concord to retrieve his own Winchester and the Remington. 'Something I never knew there was.'

'What you talkin' about, mister?' a voice shouted after him as he crossed the track.

He spat a stream of saliva far ahead. 'Whore with a heart of gold.'

The George G. Gilman Appreciation Society

**PLEASE NOTE that
THE GEORGE G. GILMAN
APPRECIATION SOCIETY**
will now be operating from
**Mr MICHAEL STOTTER,
42 Halstead Road, London, E.11. 2AZ.**

NEL

21

YEARS

BESTSELLERS

T035 794	HOW GREEN WAS MY VALLEY	Richard Llewellyn	95p
T039 560	I BOUGHT A MOUNTAIN	Thomas Firbank	90p
T033 988	IN THE TEETH OF THE EVIDENCE	Dorothy L. Sayers	90p
T040 755	THE KING MUST DIE	Mary Renault	85p
T038 149	THE CARPETBAGGERS	Harold Robbins	£1.50
T040 917	TO SIR WITH LOVE	E. R. Braithwaite	75p
T041 719	HOW TO LIVE WITH A NEUROTIC DOG	Stephen Baker	75p
T040 925	THE PRIZE	Irving Wallace	£1.60
T034 755	THE CITADEL	A. J. Cronin	£1.10
T034 674	STRANGER IN A STRANGE LAND	Robert A. Heinlein	£1.20
T037 673	BABY & CHILD CARE	Dr Benjamin Spock	£1.50
T037 053	79 PARK AVENUE	Harold Robbins	£1.25
T035 697	DUNE	Frank Herbert	£1.25
T035 832	THE MOON IS A HARSH MISTRESS	Robert A. Heinlein	£1.00
T040 933	THE SEVEN MINUTES	Irving Wallace	£1.50
T038 130	THE INHERITORS	Harold Robbins	£1.25
T035 689	RICH MAN, POOR MAN	Irwin Shaw	£1.50
T037 134	EDGE 27: DEATH DRIVE	George G. Gilman	75p
T037 541	DEVIL'S GUARD	Robert Elford	£1.25
T038 386	THE RATS	James Herbert	75p
T030 342	CARRIE	Stephen King	75p
T033 759	THE FOG	James Herbert	80p
T033 740	THE MIXED BLESSING	Helen Van Slyke	£1.25
T037 061	BLOOD AND MONEY	Thomas Thompson	£1.50

NEL P.O. BOX 11, FALMOUTH TR10 9EN, CORNWALL.

Postage charge

U.K. Customers: Please allow 22p for the first book plus 10p per copy for each additional book ordered to a maximum charge of 82p to cover the cost of postage and packing.

B.F.P.O. & Eire: Please allow 22p for the first book plus 10p per copy for the next 6 books, thereafter 4p per book.

Overseas Customers: Please allow 30p for the first book plus 10p per copy for each additional book.

Please send cheque or postal order (no currency).

Name ....

Address ....

....

Title ....

While every effort is made to keep prices steady, it is sometimes necessary to increase prices at short notice. New English Library reserve the right to show on covers and charge new retail prices which may differ from those advertised in the text or elsewhere.